FLIGHTS OF A COAST DOG

Jack Schofield

FLIGHTS OF A COAST DOG

A Pilot's Log

DOUGLAS & McINTYRE
Vancouver / Toronto

Previous page: A pilot's view of Knight Inlet, B.C. BRIAN SCHOFIELD PHOTO

Copyright © 1999 by Jack Schofield

99 00 01 02 03   5 4 3 2 1

Douglas & McIntyre Ltd.
2323 Quebec Street, Suite 201
Vancouver, British Columbia
V5T 4S7

Canadian Cataloguing in Publication Data

Schofield, Jack
  Flights of a coast dog

  ISBN 1-55054-677-5

  1. Schofield, Jack   2. Bush pilots—British Columbia—Biography.   3. Pacific Coast (B.C.)—Biography.   I. Title.
TL540.S36A3   1999   629.13'092   C99-910017-3

Editing by John Eerkes
Front jacket photograph by Tom Langdon
Back jacket photograph by Brian Schofield
Design and typesetting by Val Speidel
Printed and bound in Canada by Friesens
Printed on acid-free paper ∞

Care has been taken to trace the ownership of the illustrations used in this book. The publisher welcomes any information that will enable it to correct any errors or omissions in future editions.

The publisher gratefully acknowledges the assistance of the Canada Council for the Arts and of the British Columbia Ministry of Tourism, Small Business and Culture. The publisher also acknowledges the financial support of the Government of Canada through the Book Publishing Industry Development Program for its publishing activities.

CONTENTS

PREFACE

Seaplane pilots flying on the coast of British Columbia refer to their daily job as 95 percent boredom and 5 percent sheer terror. This typical understatement might appear to be true to someone perusing dry, mathematical entries in an aircraft journey logbook, but the pilot's personal recollections often tell a different story.

The events described in this book occurred during my too-brief flying career as a charter seaplane pilot operating in the B.C. mid-coast area from the 1960s to the 1980s. The people encountered in these pages are real and are identified here with the great affection one assigns to those who shared moments from the past. I am indebted to all those whose presence and actions contributed to the events described here, and no malice is stated or implied.

It is my good fortune to have a continuing role in the aviation industry as editor of *West Coast Aviator* magazine, in whose pages three of these stories first appeared under the title "Hurry Up and Wait." Several of my drawings, used here as illustrations, will be familiar to local aviators, as will the Port Hardy mural, which continues to hang in that city's airport terminal and is reproduced on the endpapers of this book. Many of the two hundred pilots whose names appear on this painting are now, or have been, captains with major airlines. To a man, they look back on their days "on floats" as the highlight of an adventure with airplanes. If there is a dedication to be made for this book, it is to all who have been so anointed—past, present and future floatplane pilots.

THE BAT AND TWO KITCHEN CHAIRS

My friend Kenny and I used to ride our bikes out to Vancouver airport. In those days it was called Sea Island airport, and what we now call the South Terminal was where all the action took place. There was nothing happening over on the north side, except for what cows do.

From our homes in Kerrisdale we would speed down Granville Street, past Eburne Sawmills and over the old Marpole swing bridge. If anything bigger than a rowboat was going down the river, that bridge would swing open and we would wait for what seemed an eternity for it to close, before heading along Airport Road to the airfield.

The main attraction for these two ten-year-old kids was an aircraft we called "the Bat." CF-BAT was a low-wing monoplane with a ninety-horse Warner radial engine. She was a fabric-covered plane sporting a brilliant yellow doped finish with black trim and speed lines.

The cockpit was a side-by-side arrangement for pilot and passenger, and access was through a forward-swinging canopy.

Kenny and I would join the "bicycle brigade" at the fence in front of Gilbert's Flying School. There were always several other kids at the fence who became our immediate allies in a shared affection for the Bat. We would press our faces against the wire-mesh fence and marvel at the sheer beauty of this little aeroplane.

In those days there were no "Wichita Cream Puffs," with their tricycle gear; every plane was a "tail-dragger" and stood its ground like an aeroplane should—with its nose pointed skyward. The Bat had something special about its stance that set it apart from all other planes on the field—it had "pants." We would later learn that the correct terminology was "wheel fairing," but we in the gallery had our own way to describe the rakish beauty these cosmetic devices bestowed upon the Bat.

Burned into our young memories is the scenario that would unfold before our eager, envious eyes on those many sunny days at the fence: a man would slide expertly into the Bat's cockpit, often followed by a young, blonde woman, who sat in the right-hand passenger seat. Another man, in white coveralls, would saunter toward the Bat from the direction of the hangar (we later discovered that all mechanics saunter). The engineer would call out as he approached the plane, "Switches off—Brakes set!"

The hero in the cockpit would acknowledge that, indeed, the switches were off and the brakes were set. "White Coveralls" would grasp the shiny, varnished wooden propeller with both his hands on the uppermost blade. He would bring his chest right up against the propeller and then, in one fluid movement, snap the prop downward while stepping back out of the way. He would do this four times; each time the engine would let out a puff, and then he would call out, "Brakes set—Switches on—Contact!" Our hero in the cockpit would acknowledge this command by repeating it very clearly: "Brakes set, switches on—Contact!"

Again, the fluid action of the

mechanic brought him back from the now-living propeller as the engine coughed into life. Smoke from the reluctant motor was picked up by the whirling prop and swept across the tarmac toward us at the fence. We all inhaled as one.

To provide the pilot with vision over its high nose, the Bat would have to zigzag along the tarmac as it taxied out to the runway. At the intersection the yellow plane would stop, awaiting an Aldis light signal from the control tower. A green light was flashed and acknowledged by a wag from the Bat's rudder; then the plane trundled across the runway to the grass infield area for takeoff. The blonde woman's hair blew into the slipstream as the canopy was closed and the Bat turned into wind. We never gave that pretty girl a second's thought, for we were ten and in love with an aeroplane called the Bat.

When airport trips were rained out or when parents got difficult, Kenny and I would retire to the basement of my family home. We would place two kitchen chairs side by side and pull an old tarpaulin over our heads. Using a toilet plunger as a joystick and simulating the roar of the Bat with an ample spray of saliva, we would fly off into a world of our own.

Many years later, while I was ramping my seaplane at Vancouver airport, a once-familiar voice hailed me. It was my old friend, Kenny. How strange it was to meet again in a spot less than a hundred feet from where we two, as kids, had watched the Bat taxi out for takeoff.

Ken told me that in those intervening years since biking to the airport, he had become very successful in business. Finding himself with money and time to spare, he had turned to an old yearning—he had bought an airplane and had learned to fly.

I have never flown with Ken in his new plane, but he must be a great pilot, because he could always make it over my mother's old Bluebird washing machine in those days when we "flew the Bat in the basement" into the wild blue yonder of our imaginations.

1
OQU – Selling to Fly

The cardboard tube lashed to the float struts was getting soaked. Peering out at it from the water-streaked pilot's window of the little Cessna, I could see the tube getting mushy and coming apart from the effects of the slipstream and the driving rain. Inside that tube were three marine antennas destined for my first stop at the Minstrel Island general store. If the cardboard unravelled completely the eight-foot-long antennas would end up in Johnstone Strait, some fifty feet below me. The thought strayed through my mind that I would, in future, fibreglass one of those big tubes and fasten it permanently to the float struts, but right now I was too busy skinning under the power lines that spanned Discovery Passage to worry about my external load.

The three big orange balls fastened to the power lines were to my left and slightly above me as my little Cessna 172 bucked and yawed under the high-voltage span. I hated flying under

power lines. It gave me a puckered feeling—a gigantic updraft could lift me into the 23,000-volt wires. Each time I flew under these wires I was reminded of the story told by local pilots of a Beaver flying into the stringing cables when B.C. Hydro were installing this cable crossing. The aircraft took the stringing wires across the forward float struts, causing it to perform an outside loop and end up on the water with its pontoons driven up under its wings. All aboard were badly shaken but survived.

Ahead, on the left, I could make out the entrance to Brown's Bay, and to my right, a mere blur in the heavy rain, was the eastern shoreline of the strait. The ceiling was down to about two hundred feet with ragged wisps of grey crud blowing past me at a hundred and fifty feet, where, now that I was clear of the wires, I had levelled off.

My little seaplane was red and white, like every other Cessna off the Wichita, Kansas, assembly line. This one was a

1

1963 Cessna 172. It was mounted on what are referred to as CAP 2000 floats and performed rather minimally as a seaplane. The 145-horse, six-cylinder Continental engine threw a fixed-pitch propeller that was designed as a compromise between the required pitch for takeoff, climb and cruise requirements. Although my little bird was not quick off the water, once in the air, with any kind of a load aboard, it flew along at about 110 miles an hour, and like all Cessnas was a very forgiving little airplane. What made it a truly wonderful craft was the fact that it was all mine—notwithstanding a bank loan of $8,200.

CF-OQU was ten years old on this very day, and she had come out of the water at Campbell River with a load of two huge videotape recorders, ten citizens' band radio sets, a couple of portable record players, a pile of electronic bits and pieces and the three antennas strapped to the float struts.

On the back seat there was an electronic-parts catalogue about a foot thick (and weighing a ton), along with a soft overnight bag with my change of underwear. I was a travelling salesman for an electronics supply company, and my territory was "anywhere in British Columbia, so long as it was between Victoria and Prince Rupert." I featured myself as something of a trend setter in those days. I was, after all, the only travelling salesman who ever called on the stores at Blind Bay or Minstrel Island or Echo Bay.

"There's a real need for a little airline around here." Ed Carder, the new owner of Minstrel Island, was planning his future. "I figure one day I'll start one right here out of Minstrel, but for now I've got my hands full getting this place in shape," he said, gesturing to the store and the complex of piers and docks.

Minstrel was a pretty disreputable-looking place at this time. The docks, the pier and the hotel were all relics of the island's former days of grandeur, when Union Steamships served the coast. Those famous black-and-red-funnelled steamers had made Minstrel Island a major community before the airlines took over transportation into this country. Passengers from the many logging camps and villages in the area would assemble here to await freight

With CF-OQU during my flying-salesman years. The aircraft is a Cessna 172 powered with a 145-horsepower Continental engine—not a brilliant performer as a floatplane.

2

Minstrel Island, where I first met Ed and Margit Carder while selling them marine radios and electronics. The 1904 hotel is pictured here, but the general store had burned down before this photo was taken.
BRIAN SCHOFIELD PHOTO

and other passengers coming up from Vancouver. The hotel, now leaning into the hill for support, once provided the necessary amenities for waiting steamship passengers, who could drink themselves into oblivion at the bar and then sleep it off in one of the twenty-six rooms of the 1904-vintage building.

"I'm going to rebuild this pier, replace or repair all those floats and turn this place into a resort. There will be boat gas, diesel and avgas. Minstrel will be back to its former self," boasted the young American, who had arrived only two months before, out of the blue, from Tacoma.

Ed Carder had bought the entire island and moved in with his wife and two young boys. Although his plans sounded pretty ambitious, Ed had already refurbished the general store, stocking it to the gunwales, and was doing a heavy volume of business in

groceries and general supplies. His wife, Margit, and the two boys looked after the store while Ed rebuilt a big net shed into living accommodation for his family. The many pleasure boats and commercial craft cruising these waters would soon learn that Minstrel was a good place to stop for provisions.

Maybe Ed is just the person to bring Minstrel Island back to life, I thought as I taxied out of the little bay. I was not to know until much later that my pleasant, friendly acquaintance would play a significant role in my future here on the mid-coast. This energetic young man would become the principal player in what was to be one of the most bizarre incidents ever to occur on the mid-coast: his actions would, at a later date, alter my life considerably.

I pulled up the water rudders and firewalled the throttle. CF-OQU, the registered ident of my little plane, lifted

Fuelling at Porpoise Bay on the way up the coast on a sales trip. BRIAN SCHOFIELD PHOTO

off the water lighter by five CB sets and those antennas and by the gas burned during the flight up from Campbell River. She poked her nose into Knight Inlet and climbed into the tailwind offered by the outflowing sou'easter.

My sales trips would take me on to Echo Bay in Simoom Sound and then over to Alert Bay, where I would refuel before proceeding to Port McNeill and Port Hardy. Sometimes I would fly over to Sullivan Bay for the night, then on up the coast to Bella Bella and Ocean Falls, continuing on to Prince Rupert. On other occasions, I would stay over in Port McNeill and jam all night with a friend who played great jazz piano—

my trumpet was always tucked under the electronic stuff in the back of the plane.

At each stop I would call on the stores, the radio/TV repairman and the schools (if there were any). The sale of CB radios and antennas was quite active because the many fishboats in the area were installing these radios. They were a boon to the loggers and floatcamps, providing everybody with cheap, and occasionally effective, communication. The school districts were very excited about the recent Japanese development of the helical scan videotape recorder, and I demonstrated these up and down the coast with pretty good results.

Video technology was very new in the 1970s, but I figured that one day it would be a major industry, with pre-recorded tapes available for entertainment and education. The recorders I sold for educational use were reel-to-reel machines using half-inch magnetic tape that recorded in black and white only—colour and the videocassette would come much later.

In addition to selling to the school boards, I got the idea of setting up some kind of mini-TV entertainment system with the logging camps, whose men were starved for something to do in the evenings during their fourteen-day stint in camp. Although my vision was accurate, my concept was ahead of its day.

"Fly us in some tapes of movies and TV shows" was the plea of those bored, camp-bound loggers. The idea of canned entertainment during the long winter nights appealed to these men, and I figured I was on to something big. It sounded like a great way to make money, but there was a hitch: it was illegal. To record broadcasted programs for resale was a breach of copyright. Also, the ever-creative loggers wanted the commercials removed, and, "While you're at it, how about some blue movies?" I decided not to get involved. A friend in the cable TV business came up with a better idea.

"Why not offer the logging camps their own cable TV system?" queried my friend, Walter Green, the systems engineer for Alberni Cablevision. Walter was an avid glider pilot and would make any excuse to go flying—he could smell a flying trip up the coast. "I'd be happy to teach you how to install the systems, and the camp could either feed it with an off-air signal or hook in a video playback unit. Stay away from the programming, and supply just the system." It was a great idea, and Walter got his trip up the coast.

We installed a mini-system at Scott Cove, in Simoom Sound, and located a signal from Channel 2 atop a little bluff at the entrance to the cove. Although the signal strength from the antenna was almost nonexistent, the loggers loved it. The bunkhouse and cookhouse were hooked up, as were the many private homes on floats in the bay. I was now a semi-qualified cable installer and took off in my little plane to find other prospects. Alas, someone with fewer scruples than I was already supplying many of the camps with videotapes illegally recorded off the air, from Vancouver stations. He also edited out the commercials. The logging companies bought the reel-to-reel video player and put it in the recreation hall, where the men assembled to watch the

6

Left: The scene that greeted me following a flash snowstorm in Deep Bay, near Qualicum Beach. The airplane rolled over at the dock from the weight of snow on its wings and tailplane.

Right: The seiner *Sea Luck* lifts OQU from the waters of Deep Bay. The aircraft was "inched" to the surface, allowing the water to drain slowly from its wings in order to avoid structural damage.

most recent movies, which were flown in daily by the company plane. I once visited Weldwood's Thompson Sound operation, where the men were watching a popular sitcom. At the end of this tape, the supplier had slipped in some choice scenes from *Deep Throat*. That was a hard act to follow, so I went back to selling CB radios and school audio-video equipment.

One very black, overcast morning, I left my home at Qualicum Beach and headed over to Port Alberni by car. Before reaching Cathedral Grove, I ran into a snowstorm. The flakes were so large and wet that I became concerned about my airplane, which had been left at Deep Bay near my home. I wheeled around and headed back, concerned that the buildup of snow on the aircraft could sink her at the dock. The road, so recently travelled,

was now covered with two inches of slush, and the storm became very intense as I sped back along the highway. Arriving at the Little Qualicum River crossing, I was dismayed to find a lineup of cars unable to move past a Greyhound bus, which was lying on its side across the road. The bus had slid into a telephone pole and the power and telephone lines were down. A policeman told me it would be at least two hours before traffic could get through. I was stopped dead in my tracks, unable to move and unable to phone ahead to warn someone to sweep off the plane before it sank. Destiny was at work.

Eventually I made it, on foot, to Deep Bay. I stood on the rickety, snow-covered wharf, looking sadly at the tip of OQU's wing, which barely protruded from the frozen water. "We didn't know what to do. The tail went down under

A fine catch. The insurance company was going to write OQU off, even though it had only minor water damage. I bid on the repair job and got the contract.

the weight of the snow, and she slowly rolled over at the dock," said the distressed lady who had watched the whole thing from her kitchen window. OQU was in deep water and was being held, upside down, against the dock by her still-buoyant floats. The ropes holding the plane in place were as tight as bowstrings. It was a very sad sight.

Dave Nilson, the chief engineer with Island Airlines, was on his way down from Campbell River to arrange the salvage, and Mark Recalma had volunteered his sixty-foot seiner, *Sea Luck*, to handle the lifting job. It was a textbook operation, as both men knew their business. The plane was held off from the ship as the outswung boom was winched upward, hauling the plane slowly from the water. The operation paused frequently to allow the water in the wings to drain out for fear of structural damage from the weight of the trapped water. OQU came out of the frozen bay looking for all the world like a flyable airplane. She was set back gently onto her pontoons, and as I broke the surface ice with a flailing paddle, she was inched back to the dock.

"Pull all the instruments and all the radios and throw them in that bucket of fresh water," Nilson instructed as he removed the cowlings to get at the magnetos and drain out the contaminated oil. As I proceeded to do as

instructed, Dave removed both magnetos and poured diesel oil into the crankcase. He pulled the prop through to fully inhibit the cylinders and then placed all the spark plugs and the magnetos into a box. "Put these in a four-hundred-degree oven overnight," he said. "I'll be back in the morning. We'll get her fired up and fly back to Campbell River." Both of us were shivering from the experience, and it took no prompting to head home.

The next morning, with the "mags" back in place and the crankcase filled with clean oil, a battery jury-rigged into place and the fuel system purged of water, Dave started the six-cylinder Continental with little difficulty. He didn't waste time and took off from the bay with a company escort plane in hot pursuit. As I watched him climb into the clear, cold sky, I started to understand that airplanes were not all fun and games.

"We're going to write it off," the insurance adjuster said over the phone. I couldn't believe my ears as he explained: "The plane is insured for only $13,000. The engine has only fifty hours to go before it is time-expired. The lowest bid we have for the repair is over $20,000, so we're going to write it

The "new look" of the little Cessna after the Avcon conversion. The 145-horsepower engine was replaced with 180 horses and a constant-speed propeller. The little "blisters" on the side of the cowlings made room for the slightly larger engine.

off and pay out the $13,000." He went on to inform me that had they received a bid as low as $13,000 for the repairs, they would have repaired it; otherwise, goodbye OQU. I solved his problem by submitting my own bid of $13,000 and was awarded the contract.

Bidding on my own plane's repair proved to be a very wise move. Despite having little mechanical training, I did a lot of the work myself and farmed out the rest to qualified people. All the instruments and radios were replaced with new ones, and I bought a low-time Lycoming 180-horsepower engine and an Avcon conversion kit that included a constant-speed prop. This additional power would make my little bird perform more like a Cessna 180, I figured. It took me seven months to perform the conversion, but the real delays were caused by the engineer who inspected and signed out my work. He kept taking off to places unknown, and the few times I saw him he wanted money for work he had not completed. I finally got fed up with him and arranged for George Bignall, a very experienced engineer living in Qualicum Beach, to perform the hard work. I took on the rewiring of the aircraft myself and completely gutted the old wiring. This was a big job for a novice, but I learned a lot about that airplane.

When we launched OQU back into

the water at French Creek, she had thirty-five more horses up front, a constant-speed prop, new radios, new upholstery and a super flight panel—all for a total cost of $8,000 and seven months of my spare time. Financially speaking, it was the best thing that an airplane ever did for me, because I had pocketed $5,000 of the insurance payment for my troubles.

With the new engine and prop, OQU performed like a champion. She was particularly good at getting out with a load, and although the cruising speed did not increase more than eight miles per hour, the constant-speed prop gave smooth and economical power. All I needed now was enough business to keep her flying.

The Qualicum Beach airport, where I had rebuilt the plane, was a dirt strip at this time, in 1969. The very active flying club there was trying to convince the city fathers that an airport made sense for a tourism-oriented community. One of the big players in this effort was Bill Fouty, who had started a little charter operation called Aquila Air. Bill's airline had only one plane, a Cessna 172 on wheels, but he was looking for a chance to grow.

I mentioned to Bill that a seaplane operation somewhere near Sullivan Bay would be a winner because the traditional airline in that area, Alert Bay Air

Services (ABAS), had moved to Port Hardy airport on Vancouver Island, leaving the people on the mainland mid-coast without a close local service. Bill became very interested and made arrangements to fly up north with me on my next selling trip. He had obtained expert advice that it was legal for him to position an airplane at a remote base and charge the same tariffs as those in place for his Qualicum airline. (This premise was the subject of intense debate among other airlines at a later date, when we were accused of being a quasi-legal "chisel charterer," but the Canadian Transport Commission, a horse's-ass of a committee operated by parliamentary appointees, was advised of the situation and never instructed Bill otherwise.)

Bill and I took off one magnificent spring day and headed up the coast to check out the possibilities. He was a little skeptical at the beginning, but the fine flying weather and the awe-inspiring country soon won him over. "I'm prepared to put a 180 on floats up here, but you'd better be prepared to live up here and fly it," he announced.

"What the hell," I replied, casting my usual sagacity to the wind. "Let's do it."

So we did it, and that's how I became a coast charter pilot. At that time, I had no more than a thousand hours' total flying time, six hundred of it on floats. I was also a little older than most beginners, but like most fledgling pilots I figured I was an ace—it wouldn't be long before I would learn the correct spelling and pronunciation of that word.

Our new venture didn't come together immediately; a plane had to be located and purchased, and some form of accommodation needed to be arranged. We would need a radio phone at our remote base because there were no land lines in the area. We soon found that it was one thing to see the opportunity and another to get our little airline into operation—but it was fun.

In our earlier travels around Simoom Sound, checking out possible base locations, we had met a family in a place called Shawl Bay. Alan and Edna Brown suggested that we tie up on their float-camp and base our airline out of their home. It proved to be an excellent choice; Alan had lived in this country for thirty-five years, knew the winds and tides and waterways and was familiar with everyone who lived here. He proved to be a never-ending source of information and good advice, while Shawl Bay proved to be an all-weather place, very kind to floatplanes in any wind or sea.

Bill Fouty located a Cessna 180 on Edo 2760s (2760 is the displacement in pounds of water that each float will handle, similar to a ship's tonnage). CF-BIU was a low-time airplane in excellent condition. She was distinctive from other 180s in one respect—her paint job. She had been a deep, shiny maroon colour at the factory, but sun and sea had changed all that and the paint had chalked and turned quite dark. Later, the Native people at Kingcome village would call her "the black airplane" because she appeared black from the ground as we banked over the village, signalling our arrival.

Bill was in his element with this new business. He was a quiet man, somewhat shy in a group, but a doer and a great practical organizer. He was in his glory when building or fixing things. He had located a small, thirty-foot retired fuel barge and had replanked the

The Island Airlines dock at the Campbell River spit in the early 1970s. A now-extinct Fairchild Husky occupies the centre position on the dock. TOM LANGDON COLLECTION

Sointula, located on Malcolm Island, was a regular stop for OQU. The sale of citizens' band radios to the many fishermen living here was the main attraction during my salesman years. Later, the village became a scheduled stop for the airline. PHOTO COURTESY ULLI STELTZER, FROM *COAST OF MANY FACES*

bottom, gutted it of all the pipes and tanks, redecked it and built a house on it fit for a king, or at least fit for a pilot in the boonies. There must have been a sale on "olive drab" paint because that's what he painted her, from stem to gudgeon—olive green. Ugly, maybe, but equipped for comfort with a propane hot-water tank, oven and stove, a shower stall, a sitting room and a separate bedroom equipped with two bunks, complete with five-inch foam mattresses. "Tight as a bull's ass in fly time," he quipped as he fibreglassed the roof. She would prove to be just that when the monsoon-like rainfall of the north coast hammered her later in Shawl Bay.

While all this building was going on, I was flying the company Cessna 172 on the very few charter trips generated out of Qualicum Beach. When not flying, I would help out in building the barge house and did a little running around down to Quesnel Lake, near Nanaimo, where the new seaplane was getting put into shape by engineer George Bignall. These were happy days, filled with the adventure of a new enterprise and the anticipation of getting paid for doing what we all loved to do—fly airplanes.

We launched "the Green Thing," as Edna Brown called it, and it sailed north from French Creek behind the troller owned by Bill's business partner. "Sailed" is a misnomer, for it wallowed along behind the fishboat, taking the wind on its slab side and yawing off, crosswind, in a very unseaworthy manner. It was tough to tow up Johnstone Strait, but for Bill and me, anticipating our new adventure, she looked like the *Queen Mary* on her maiden voyage.

2

BIU – Shawl Bay

The rain hammered against the wall of the little barge, and rivulets of water ran off the fibreglass roof onto the deck. The "slap" of the pools of rainwater spilling from the cambered deck into the sea had awakened me. Though still fighting sleep, I was conscious of the sounds of something more than a summer storm as the waves rocked my floating home. On this pre-dawn morning, a driving wind was carrying heavy rain down onto the wings of the Cessna 180 seaplane tied up outside, not half a wingspan from where I slept. The sporadic drumming of the rain across the top of the wings added a new note to the age-old symphony played by wind and wave in the wilderness of the B.C. coast.

Without leaving my warm bunk I trained a flashlight through the window and illuminated the inboard wing tip of CF-BIU, our only plane. The tip was scribing a one-foot arc as the slop from Kingcome Inlet found its way into our safe harbour and rocked the plane against its mooring.

It must be really blowing out there, I thought, for it took storm-force winds to cause any movement to the water here in Shawl Bay. With any luck I'll get the day off, I mused, covering my head with the pillow in what I knew would be a vain attempt to drown out the impending "blat" of that dreaded telephone horn out on the dock. Warm and dry in my little barge house and with the prospect of a day off from what had become a mad schedule of flying duties, I rolled over and in a half-sleep relished memories of our adventures so far.

To get our business started, Bill Fouty had moved to Shawl Bay to help me organize the operations of the base and also to enable us to spell each other off with the flying. The telephone company had installed a radio phone in the Browns' kitchen and mounted the antennas on the roof of

B. SCHOFIELD – '84

Shawl Bay from the air. A southeast wind blew out of the bay while a westerly blew in one side and then out the other, making it always possible to land into wind. BRIAN SCHOFIELD PHOTO

their house. When the phone rang it actuated a claxon on the dock that was so loud it scared the hell out of every seagull for miles around while alerting us, in the barge, of an impending trip. Radio phones are assigned an alphabetically designated channel. Ours was on J channel, and all conversations were broadcast in plain language to everyone from Kelsey Bay in the south to Smith Sound in the north: everybody knew our business, and we knew theirs. Listening in on the conversations of some logger phoning his sweetheart from camp or overhearing Nancy from Echo Bay chatting with her family

down south was a popular form of entertainment where the TV reception was unreliable at best.

The B.C. Tel installation crew warned us that reception in the back of the bay would vary with the effects of "atmospherics." They were right: some days the radio phone would work fine, but on other days voices would fade off or the phone would ring with nothing audible on the other end. Alan Brown became our dispatcher, and thanks to his tenacity and cunning we rarely missed a trip due to atmospherics. When something went amiss in the communications, Alan would call another station to ask whether they had heard who had called us. At other times, when someone couldn't get through, the operator at nearby Scott Cove or Echo Bay would come on the line: "Hey, Kingcome wants an airplane right away."

The lack of privacy on the radio phone was a problem for some people, but for our little airline it proved to be the best advertising we could get. The busier we became, the more people in the area knew we were around. We got busier and busier, rarely arriving back at home base before dark each day. We had a VHF aircraft band transmitter at Shawl Bay, which allowed the plane to monitor the company frequency of 122.85 for new instructions. When we

The Brown family's floatcamp at Shawl Bay. Their home is the largest of the buildings. The family had lived in this camp for thirty-five years, though not always in this location. BRIAN SCHOFIELD PHOTO

were out of radio range, Alan would call our next destination to leave further information. This "moccasin telegraph" system worked better than state-of-the-art electronics.

Bill Fouty was a fairly low-time pilot with zero time on floats. But he was a natural with machines of any kind and a very conscientious pilot, so nobody was at risk flying with Bill. Despite this, he knew that we were flying in some of the toughest floatplane country on the coast, and he found it nerve-racking. When the claxon sounded on the dock and it was his turn to fly, Bill would feel this big grip on his guts. He would

tense up and worry his way through the day's flying duties, relaxing only at nightfall when nobody could make him do it again. One day Alan Brown, having a wicked sense of humour, short-circuited the phone horn and virtually blew Bill right out the door. The "blat" of the phone caught Bill snoozing. Wearing only his socks and underwear, he shot out the door of the pilot's barge and slid on the wet dock almost into the water. Alan and Edna Brown were doubled over in laughter, as was I, but Bill was some ticked off.

The next morning I woke up, on the top bunk, to Bill's exclamation from the bottom bunk: "What the hell am I

15

16

doing here? I own this bloody airline. I can do what I want. I'm going home." All of us at Shawl Bay had a good laugh over Bill's self-revelation, and in a couple of days he did go home. I flew him back to Deep Bay, near Qualicum Beach, and returned to Shawl Bay to be the one-man airline that we had originally planned.

The Native village at Kingcome, located only ten minutes away, became our best customer. Their phone call with instructions to "send Jack for three to Alert Bay" became commonplace, and my logbook attests to as many as seven calls in one day into the village. Our very first charter had been out of Kingcome and it had proven memorable. The call came in ten minutes after the B.C. Tel installation crew had left Shawl Bay. We were standing

around admiring our new radio phone when the claxon went off right in our faces. Startled, Alan answered. "Three out of Kingcome to Alert," he called to me, grinning as he hung up. It was my turn in the barrel, so I fired up BIU and Bill turned me out with a farewell slap on the elevators.

As I taxied out of the inner bay toward the big rock for that first charter, I felt apprehensive. There is a difference between flying for hire, at someone else's bidding, and taking off of your own volition. This thought struck me as I firewalled the throttle, commencing the takeoff. Flying low, up Kingcome Inlet past Wakeman Sound, there was a special thrill, a mixture of dread and joy. Dread, that I might do something wrong; joy, that at long last I was doing exactly what I had wanted to do since soloing in a Tiger Moth way back in 1946.

My fear of not measuring up was well placed, because I was about to pull off a dumb trick. What I didn't know was that local pilots did not land at the village, despite all assurances from the customer. The Kingcome River is an underwater stump farm in the area adjacent to Kingcome village. It was usual for customers from Kingcome village to motorboat downriver to the dock at the logging camp, where the plane could land safely. Fortunately my

The swift Kingcome River, as seen from the beach at the village. On the opposite bank, immediately above the canoe's bow, is where I took my swim to recover the fast-drifting airplane. The river at this location is still affected by tide; low tide reveals many stumps and logs, which are hazardous to manoeuvring aircraft. PHOTO COURTESY ULLI STELTZER, FROM *COAST OF MANY FACES*

landing occurred at high tide, when the tidal inflow raised the river well above the hidden snags. Landing with the confidence of the ignorant, I searched the village shoreline for a dock. There didn't appear to be one. I looked for some kind of place to tie up, but all that presented itself was a mud flat upon which the village canoes were beached. I became the subject of some amused finger-pointing by some of the village children before I suddenly spied something on the opposite side of the river from the village. Almost totally hidden by overhanging trees was a dock with a large fishboat tied up to it.

Since there was plenty of space behind the boat I glided alongside, shut off the engine and stepped quickly ashore with my aft rope in hand. This rope was twenty feet long and

not much thicker than binder twine. I searched the dock for a bollard or tie-down rail, but there was nothing— nowhere to tie my rope, not even a space between the planks. Meanwhile the swift current streaming from beneath the dock suddenly swept the bow of BIU's floats out into the running stream. I fought to hold the plane against the current while, on the aft deck of the fishboat, a Native gentleman sat reading. He must have recognized my plight, but did nothing except watch me attempt to pull the plane back to the dock against a nine-knot current.

I was, by this time, truly reaching the end of my rope. Poor Bill, I thought, was about to lose his new airplane on its very first paying trip. The thought of reporting such a

BIU – SHAWL BAY

The Kingcome villagers asked us to "buzz" their soccer field to alert them that we were about to land, downstream, at the seaplane dock.

life in such an unlikely event, had remained in the baggage compartment because it was too warm to wear on such a grand day.

My passengers, now on the dock, were laughing and waving me back. I taxied back, and they all caught the lift strut and held BIU tight against the dock's brow log. The gentleman on the fishboat was still watching me with something less than amusement. Standing there, making a big puddle on the dock, I asked him about the lack of tie-downs and why he hadn't helped me out. He informed me, with great aplomb and in a totally inoffensive manner, that this was a private dock; he did not invite me to use it, and his was the only craft in need of cleats, which he was using to secure his own vessel. Further, I was told, no knowledgeable seaplane pilot lands at the village, but downstream at the logging company's seaplane dock. "Have a pleasant flight," the gentleman said as we cast off.

Much later, I would meet Chief Dave Dawson Senior under more convivial circumstances. We had a good laugh over this event, which he recalled with great amusement. What I had not known at the time was that all my passengers were members of the Willie family, of whom the Dawson family were not totally enamoured. From that date

catastrophe drove me to a desperate act. Winding the remainder of the rope around my hand and clutching it with all my strength, I jumped into the raging water and pulled myself, hand over hand, under the surface, until I reached the plane. The moment I felt the rope end at the float strut I was up into the cockpit, cranking the engine over faster than I would have believed possible. My underwear hadn't had time to get wet, so fast was my swim, but now a puddle was forming at my feet and my hair hung like string before my eyes. That International Orange floater jacket, the one I had bought to save my

Cessna 185 XRK under repair at Shawl Bay. The engine was suspended on a plank (under the tarpaulin) over the cabin of George Mooney's boat.

onward, I viewed with disdain any pilot stupid enough to land at the village.

One of my passengers that day was Dan Willie Junior. He laughed about my swim and warned me, "The Kingcome will get you someday, Uncle Jack." (Dan Willie was the first to call me "Uncle Jack," pronouncing the J like a Ch, and that name stuck among the members of all three local villages.) "Nobody swims the Kingcome, and

when it takes you it doesn't give you back." Young Dan Willie and his father themselves became victims of these waters, just one year later. True to its reputation, the Kingcome River never gave up their bodies.

As I lay in my bed on this windy, rainswept morning, recalling these early adventures, I marvelled at how this virtual novice had managed to stay out

BMO being lifted out
of Hardy Bay by the
packer *Harriet E.* The
aircraft had taken off
in the early morning
for Vancouver, end-
ing up at 4 P.M. at
the bottom of Hardy
Bay (an expensive
tryst).

of serious trouble. I had started off with
about the minimum flying time required
by the airlines—one thousand hours on
floats—and there had been no guiding
hand from an experienced pilot in the
area to save me from the hidden,
unrecorded hazards. Learning the hard
way was the best method, so long as
one survived the experience.

Pulling off the covers from my head,
I found the sun streaming through the
window, bathing my room in a warm
light. The horn blared from the dock
and I vaulted from the bunk, pulling on
my pants and a shirt and then flinging

myself out the door to ready the plane
for the impending trip.

"Go back and have your breakfast,"
a woman called as I appeared on the
barge deck. The squish of the float
pump working the outboard pontoon
was followed by the slap of the bilge as
it hit the water. Her bare feet and legs
showed from under the fuselage. "I'll do
the floats," came the voice from the hidden figure, obviously hunched over the
bilge pump but hidden from view by the
fuselage of the Cessna. It was Cheryl,
Alan and Edna Brown's daughter, being
a Good Samaritan. She bilged the float
compartments of each pontoon, paying
particular attention to the "step compartment," where the intricate sheet-
metal work delineated the forward-plan-
ing hull of the floats. This section of the
pontoons tended to leak the most
because of the constant stress imposed
by repeated landings and takeoffs.

Completing the job, Cheryl stowed
the pump in the baggage compartment
and performed my ritual morning fuel
test—checking for water in the gas.
"Not a drop," she told me as I polished
off my breakfast. It was an important
check and I would not ordinarily take
someone else's word for it, but Cheryl
had watched Bill and I perform the D.I.
(daily inspection) each morning and
had learned her lessons well. She
handed me the little cup used to test for

20

Buttoning-on the engine of XRK. *From the left:* Bill Fouty, the author, Alan Brown and engineer George Bignall.

water in the wing tanks and prepared to turn me out from the dock.

The flight that morning was down to Kelsey Bay, where I landed at the mouth of the swift-flowing Salmon River. Under in-flow wind conditions, which prevailed that day, one must complete the landing and be "off the step" before coming abeam the dock. The river narrowed just past the ramshackle old dock and turned abruptly in its path to the sea. If you missed the float, you had to take off again and do a go-around. The swift-running water and confined channel made it difficult to taxi or turn back.

Three young women dressed more for Vancouver than for the north coast were waiting for me in their car, parked by Bill Kelly's house at the seaplane

dock. With their high heels and short skirts, these ladies had some difficulty making it up the narrow steps on the Cessna's float struts. Once aboard, they filled the Cessna's small cabin with a heady scent of Chanel No. 5. The youngest giggled incessantly, while the one sitting up front with me extended her dainty, white-gloved hand, offering a card with instructions to take them to Lagoon Cove, where a big power cruiser awaited them.

I delivered this aromatic cargo onto the swim grid of the *Kona Wind*, a local charter boat, where the three women were greeted boisterously by an equal number of hearty American sport fishermen. I then took off for home base, checking out Ed Carder's Minstrel Island resort as my little plane was hammered heavily by what is a near-constant band of turbulence surrounding that little island. As I cut through Clio Channel into Knight Inlet, I caught a quick view of Ed's new seaplane bobbing at the dock.

Several days later I picked up these three ladies from the same swim grid and returned them to their car at Kelsey Bay. When I dropped them off they gave me their business card, in case I encountered other needy boaters. I grinned to myself on the return flight, sticking their card behind the visor and feeling like a New York taxi driver.

21

3

SULLIVAN BAY – A SAGA

Tomorrow's archaeologists will argue,
It was here, or here.
The sea denies their spade a proof.
Best they listen for a Stranraer's whisper
or a Beaver's blast,
Or, rake the ashes of my ancient heart
To find, first the laughter, then the tears,
which are this place's only artifact.

My flying life was about to pivot around a place called Sullivan Bay, where I refuelled at least once a day, sometimes catching a quick coffee before hurrying off on some urgent flight, at other times hanging around to kibitz with pilots flying up or down the coast. Located in a safe harbour on North Broughton Island, Sullivan Bay was the only fuel stop on the mainland side of the mid-coast and was a welcome respite for both pilots and passengers travelling to or from Vancouver. This ramshackle old float-camp played a major part in the events described here, so the reader will benefit from a glimpse at the fascinating early history of the place.

When I first arrived in this country as a flying salesman, Sullivan Bay was owned by Ursul and Stella Fox, who had purchased the floatcamp from people by the name of Germaine. Jack and Dorothy Germaine were famous among coast pilots and had resided at Sullivan

Bay for the past thirteen years. Ursul and Stella, on the other hand, did not have plans to stay long. They had acquired the camp with the intention of refurbishing the old place for a quick resale.

Ursul was very energetic, resourceful and perhaps a bit unscrupulous, a man whom I immediately recognized as part of the local colour. We became good friends during his relatively short stay in the country. He did sell the place and turned a tidy profit—probably the only person, up to that time, who had ever made money from the camp. The profit from the sale paid for Ursul's luxurious dream yacht, *Silver Fox*, which can still be seen plying these waters, though Ursul is, sadly, no longer at the helm.

Sullivan Bay is not a village or a town but merely a series of log floats

anchored to the beach with boom chain and held in position with stiff-legs, which keep the place from going ashore in a high wind. The logs, which provide the flotation, were once huge, first-growth trees, some of which measured five feet across the butt. The buildings were old even before they arrived at Sullivan Bay, having been previously used by logging camps as bunkhouses or storage sheds. The plumbing was minimal at best, and the electrical system was downright scary. Fresh water was piped down from a small lake above the camp, and the waste pipes from the many toilets were very short—they were simply punched through the floorboards into the deep-water bay.

A government dock and warehouse at Sullivan Bay were very well maintained by the Small Harbours Department of the federal government. This immaculate facility stood in sharp contrast to the next building in line, called the White House in celebration of having once seen a coat of paint of that colour. As is the role of its counterpart in Washington, D.C., the White House was always the residence of the current owner of the place. It usually sported some hanging flowerpots or other decoration that set it apart from those other faded, faintly red buildings of the camp.

A store was next in line. This building included a room set aside for the post office, which served all the residents of the immediate area from a little "pass-through" onto the wharf. Down from the store, the L-shaped dock took its immediate right turn at the back of the bay. Along this back leg were a series of buildings, each assigned a homely name describing either its appearance or its use. Chief among these were the Bay Window, the Bunkhouse, the Laundry and, at the very end of the back float, the Lodge, which was twenty-five feet wide and sixty feet long. The Lodge was always made cozy and available to wayfarers as a communal living room. This building included a good-sized, well-equipped kitchen, which had once been a logging company's cookhouse.

Every building at Sullivan Bay was independently heated by its own oil stove, whose leaky carburetors provided an eye-smarting smell of stove oil that was most apparent when you first entered the room but strangely disappeared as the night wore on and the hospitality grew. Hot water in each unit was achieved, if one displayed great patience, from a water coil that snaked within the oil stove and was connected to a galvanized water tank. No heaven, this, but an oasis in an unforgiving country where pilots and boaters could find a safe tie-up, a shower, a meal,

good company and a warm bed on a stormy night.

The history of Sullivan Bay is a two-part saga. The first part started in 1945, and the second occurred during my years in this country, 1972 to 1987. Part three is in the making; the place soldiers on as the summer home for rich American boaters, but the less glitzy history of Sullivan Bay's past contains the true heart of the place.

In the early summer months of 1946, Captain Roach of the coastal packet *Cardena* leaned over the bridge railing and called down to Myrtle Collinson, "You Sullivan Bay people are going to put us out of business!"

The young woman laughed and shouted back at him, "You'll just have to get your pilot's licence." Myrtle was working her way around the clutter of drums being unloaded from the ship onto the freight dock. The drums were marked "80–87 Avgas." From the end of the freight dock a narrow, somewhat precarious float angled off into the bay. A man with a pike pole was positioning this walkway to provide access to a T-shaped seaplane float anchored off the rock bluff at the south entrance to Sullivan Bay. Myrtle called out to him, "Bruce, do you want to try the new restaurant?" Bruce Collinson speared the pike pole into the log and walked back

26

Associated Air Taxi pilot Dennis Pierce displays a state-of-the-art pilot relief system, circa 1950. The aircraft is a rare Howard, on the way up to Kitimat. BRUCE COLLINSON COLLECTION

to join his wife. Passing the *Cardena*, the couple stopped before one of the old buildings. "I guess we should paint out that name," Bruce said, referring to the two-foot lettering on the planks that spelled out *O'Brian Bay*. That bay, whence this floatcamp had come, was now ancient history.

In the warm June of the previous year, Bruce and Myrtle Collinson had moved to Kinaird Island, where they had negotiated with old Fred Pederson for the purchase of his floatcamp anchored in O'Brian Bay. The camp had seen busier days, when Kinaird Island had been the base for the Earl and Brown Logging

Company. That logging operation had dried up and, with the loggers gone, O'Brian Bay was suddenly nowhere.

The building and floats of the camp were still in good condition, and the young couple had plans for this place. Less than a week after taking possession of the camp, Bruce and Myrtle pulled up anchor and towed their new home to Sullivan Bay, on North Broughton Island, about five miles down the inlet. Sullivan Bay afforded protection for boats, and most important to the couple's plans, seaplanes could land there. The pilot of a black Waco aircraft bearing the name "Spilsbury and Hepburn" landed around here often, servicing marine radios. The pilot, Johnny Hatch, had confirmed that aircraft could approach over the dryback (a ridge devoid of trees) between Watson and Broughton Islands when the southeasterly was blowing, and they could land from the point in a westerly wind. There had been a lot of planes in this area since the war, and Bruce figured there were going to be a lot more.

The couple secured one end of the floatcamp to the point at the south entrance to Sullivan Bay, then anchored the other end in the middle of the bay. Boat docks were located within the lee of the big camp, and seaplanes could tie up near the shore end of the floats. The old warehouse building would serve as

A famous photo, taken by Myrtle Collinson, of two Stranraer flying boats of Queen Charlotte Airlines docked nose-to-nose at Sullivan Bay. BRUCE COLLINSON COLLECTION

an ice house for Canadian Fishing Co., which had appointed Bruce as its agent, while Myrtle had reopened the post office and established the place as a point of call for Union Steamships. It was June 15, 1945, and Sullivan Bay was in business.

The *Cardena* backed away from the Sullivan Bay camp, its seasoned skipper using a minimum of reverse thrust to avoid swamping the already overloaded freight dock. A couple of people waved as the captain blew the whistle to warn that his ship was going astern. He would be pushing her hard to make the

tide for Seymour Inlet. Captain Roach wondered if those goodbye waves were somehow prophetic. Not only was the Union Steamship Company facing competition from upstart firms using cheap, retired wartime ships, but what he had said to that young woman on the dock was true: airplanes could prove to be a real threat to the familiar old black-and-red funnel.

Captain Roach's fears were well founded. Some loggers were already flying home to Vancouver on their days off. Soon, a different kind of whistle would be heard in the inlets—

Left: Pilot Ed Bray with a BC Airlines Seabee. BRUCE COLLINSON COLLECTION

Right: Every aircraft flying the coast north to Prince Rupert and the boom town of Kitimat stopped at Sullivan Bay for gas. The helicopter is Carl Agar's first one, and he brought the entire gang down to see it when it landed on the float at Sullivan Bay. The lady on the left is Myrtle Collinson; Carl Agar is in cap and sunglasses. BRUCE COLLINSON COLLECTION

the whistle through the flying wires of those unlikely flying boats, the Stranraers, of the newly formed Queen Charlotte Airlines. The multitude of wires and spars bracing the rag-wings of this great twin-engine biplane emitted a whisper that once heard would long be remembered, especially by the crews of the Union Steamships, whose scheduled calls were inevitably reduced by the "Stranny's" inimitable sigh.

The increasing frequency of the flying boats coming into Sullivan Bay posed a mixed blessing for Bruce Collinson. The ungainly craft had to be "nosed" onto the dock and the wings secured so that the wind wouldn't swing her around and throw the aircraft against a building. Secured in this manner, the big plane would "sail" the dock around against its own anchor. Also, passengers had to be put aboard from a small boat. A suitable seaplane dock

was now essential to handle not only the "Strainer," but also the increasing number of floatplanes showing up at Sullivan Bay for fuel.

The T-shaped dock was soon installed, and aircraft from several new airlines began to appear. A mixed bag of aircraft landed in those early postwar days: Norsemen, Luscombes, a PA12, a rare Howard, a Grumman Widgeon, a couple of Barkley-Grows and a gaggle of Republic Seabees. The new company names painted on these planes were Associated Air Taxi, BC Airlines and the seemingly misplaced BC Central Airways.

Although the aviation fuel business was booming, Bruce Collinson was getting a sore back from manhandling forty-five-gallon drums and pumping all that fuel by hand. The system was so slow that on many occasions five planes would be on the dock while several

Left: An early Beaver, with pilot Bernie Bergeron. Note the absence of the porthole window aft of the passenger door, signifying that this was a very low serial number DHC2. BRUCE COLLINSON COLLECTION

Right: Sullivan Bay's shuttle aircraft, a Stinson "Station Wagon," picked up passengers for the scheduled Stranraer service. BRUCE COLLINSON COLLECTION

more waited their turn by drifting around in the bay. Bruce and Myrtle contacted both Standard Oil and Imperial Oil, and a dealership was established with Standard, who installed a fuel barge for diesel fuel and hoisted a five-thousand-gallon tank atop the rock bluff over the seaplane dock. The pilots cheered the gravity-fed avgas system, and business flourished at Sullivan Bay. It had been a year since the Collinsons had moved the camp to Sullivan Bay, and they had no doubt that they had made the right move.

In those days the oil companies made a big thing about the washroom facilities at gas stations, and Sullivan Bay was no exception. A floating out-house was built adjacent to the seaplane dock. This innovation provided a two-place, nonflush system featuring a spectacular downward view of the local marine life. Very quickly named

"the Aquarium," the facility became a conversation piece for visiting pilots and passengers and remained so until environmental regulations caused it to be shut down.

Sullivan Bay was now a regular way-point on the scheduled service of Jim Spilsbury's Queen Charlotte Airlines. In 1946, Spilsbury arrived in Sullivan Bay with a proposition for the Collinsons. When he left the floatcamp later that day, Myrtle Collinson was the official agent of QCA and Sullivan Bay had one of the first radio phones in the country. In addition to having the radio phone, the camp was equipped with a ground-to-air radio system that permitted Myrtle to talk to company aircraft en route. Sullivan Bay, a mere floatcamp, was now on the map!

The growth of air traffic over the next two years changed more than the schedules of Union Steamships—it changed the lifestyle of the coast. Where once a logger or fisherman would bring his family up to be close to his work, the airplane now made it possible to commute to larger centres. The ten-days-in, four-days-out arrangement became feasible, and the loggers' trade unions were quick to bargain for such working standards.

In the past, the local camps and communities had pooled their resources and constructed a huge dance hall that was towed around the country. One week there would be a dance at Shoal Harbour, the next week at Belle-Isle. The airplane changed all that—the dancers could now whoop it up in the big city! The Coast Mission boats, which traditionally brought religion to the logging camps, found fewer and fewer places to visit, and Union Steamships made more and more cuts to its service.

Queen Charlotte Airlines soon recognized that it needed to have an aircraft based at Sullivan Bay. It positioned a four-place Stinson Voyager there, performing local charter work as well as picking up passengers around the coast and leaving them at Sullivan Bay for transfer to the "sched" flight on the Stranraers to Vancouver. This Stinson service reduced the number of points of call for the Stranraers and was so effective that it was often necessary to send another aircraft up to Sullivan Bay to help out. The Collinsons' dwelling became a post office, general store, airline waiting room and ticket office. Myrtle's mother ran the cafe, and the Collinsons' young son, Rod, was appointed head dock boy. Pumping gas, receiving freight, weighing-in passengers and baggage, docking planes, handling the mail, selling groceries and serving meals kept everyone at Sullivan Bay on the run. So busy was the fuel dock that Standard Oil installed another eight-thousand-gallon tank on the bluff.

Seaplane traffic up the coast reached its peak during the construction of the giant Kitimat-Kemano project for the Aluminum Company of Canada. Sullivan Bay experienced its busiest time during these years. By ten o'clock each morning, at least ten aircraft would have refuelled on the way up to or back from the "instant town" of Kitimat. Bruce Collinson recalled thirty-eight aircraft overnighting at Sullivan Bay one day, due to weather problems en route. "Everywhere you looked there would be a pilot rolled up on the floor, trying to sleep."

The heyday of the floatplane and the coastal airlines was highlighted by trade wars, acquisitions and takeovers. Sullivan Bay was witness to them all. Russ Baker, of the seemingly incongruous BC Central Airways, took over Associated

Three Norsemen on the dock and a Beaver drifting, awaiting a space on the gas dock. As many as thirty-eight aircraft were holed up in Sullivan Bay in one night waiting for a break in the weather. BRUCE COLLINSON COLLECTION

Air Taxi, while BC Airlines grew from Bill Sylvester's little Luscombes and Seabee aircraft to become the world's largest seaplane operation. Pacific Western Airlines was painted on the flanks of those old Stranraer flying boats and the more recent Cansos when Russ Baker made his next bid for fame by acquiring the burgeoning Queen Charlotte Airlines and establishing the first truly home-grown regional B.C. airline.

Other significant changes took place during these times: floatplanes were no longer considered fast enough for the long haul out of Vancouver, Port Hardy, Prince Rupert and the Charlottes. DC3s terminating at these major points were hauling passengers faster and in greater comfort. Floatplanes were now provid-

ing feeder service from the bush into the airports. Sullivan Bay was being phased out of the big picture.

In 1957, bored with the diminishing role of their operation, Bruce and Myrtle Collinson sold the camp to Jack and Dorothy Germaine. The Collinsons were content to leave the picturesque old buildings and floats to the hopes and dreams of others. Never again would Sullivan Bay reverberate with the familiar roar of the twin Bristol Pegasus engines of the Stranraer or the boister-ous hijinks of visiting pilots—it was time for the Collinsons to take their leave. Myrtle recalled her conviction during the early years that Sullivan Bay would be the high point in her life. It *had* been just that, and it would prove the same for others to follow.

4

BIU – Fate's Option

My working day was over, and BIU was tied up snug to the dock at Shawl Bay. The long shadows of sunset were stretching across the waters, and the sky had taken on a rosy red hue that was reflected by the glassy water of the bay and on up Kingcome Inlet—a travelogue ending to a typical summer day on the mid-coast.

The phone rang. It was Gilford village. "Please come quickly, we have an emergency. Harry James has collapsed!" Garry Brown turned me out and then jumped aboard, climbing into the right seat as the engine caught. We taxied out past the big rock for takeoff. The Cessna 180 came up on the step, knifing through the pink water. Then, breaking clear and banking around the point, we flew low across the darkening hills toward Gilford.

At the village we faced another problem. "You won't get that stretcher in this airplane," I said, attempting to stop them, but the two men ignored me

and tried to push the basket stretcher in over the top of the front passenger seat. The stretcher punched out the little Plexiglas window on the far side before I could halt them. We removed the back seat and lifted Harry out of the stretcher, making a bed for him on the floor. It was pitch black when we took off for Alert Bay.

The portside navigation light glowed red, reflecting on the underside of the wing tip, and the anti-collision light on the tail illuminated us intermittently, turning us alternately from red to black in the darkened cockpit as we sped through the gathering night. The land below, so familiar in the daytime, was now merely darker patches in the black sea. Cormorant Island loomed out of the night, and we followed the shoreline of the island around the point into a dazzle of light from Alert Bay. The street lights along the main road reflected in the water, providing a perfect flare path for the landing as our

floats kissed the water and we made the transition from airplane to motorboat, holding our breath during the touch-down against the possibility of a hidden log undoing us after such a flawless performance.

Doc Pickup was there, still wearing his slippers after having been dragged from his home—a common occurrence for him. A grocery van substituted for an ambulance. We lifted Harry from the plane to a waiting stretcher, then into the back of Shoprite's van. Doc Pickup climbed in with Harry and asked us if we were not going to stay. We said we'd return to Shawl Bay, it being a nice clear night.

"Choose your own poison," he said, closing the van door. We took off out of Alert Bay feeling a touch of "get home-itis," a killer disease among pilots, but we made it to Shawl Bay, where the surrounding mountains denied the water any reflection. Feeling for the water, I rounded out high and dropped it in, so hard that Garry's hat flew off. Although we made it, we heard that our passenger, Harry James, did not. He had died shortly after we delivered him to Alert Bay. For the next few days I flew with a piece of cardboard taped over the broken window to remind me of the frailty of man and airplanes.

There was a message waiting for me when we got in that night, to phone Bill Fouty the next morning on a land line. Something confidential was in the wind when a land line was specified, so I flew to Port McNeill early the next morning to call him. The confidential message turned out to be significant. "I've sold the airline," Bill advised me. When I recovered from this news, he suggested I give some thought to applying for my own licence out of Shawl Bay. In the meantime I was to feel free to continue flying his 180, BIU, at a special hourly lease rate until I could find another plane.

Bill also told me that the new owner was agreeable to my continued use of the airline licence until I got my own because he was interested only in the wheel-plane operation at Qualicum Beach. Bill had felt badly about selling the airline out from under me, so he made a few calls to some key people in the industry who might be interested in helping me out with a plane and financial support. In retrospect, I could have handled his selling the airline, but I never fully recovered from the help he sent me.

I ordered a coffee and sat down in the Dalewood Restaurant in Port McNeill to mull over my predicament. It was a complicated situation, so I wrote down all the problems on a paper napkin. I came to the conclusion that my biggest problem was my old friend,

Ed Carder at Minstrel Island. Ed had already applied for a class 4 air charter licence, and it was rumoured that his application would be honoured. The licence would provide him with a protected zone of twenty miles around Minstrel; no other airline could base within that zone. Shawl Bay was inside Ed's protected zone, and I had no doubt about what he would do when he was officially awarded his licence.

So, if I was to apply for a licence, it could not be from a base at Shawl Bay. The logical move would be to base out of my old watering hole, Sullivan Bay. Air charter licences took forever to obtain and required the services of a lawyer, a fair amount of cash and lots of time to lobby and prevail upon the Canadian Transport Commission, who seemed to have difficulty locating British Columbia on their maps. I would need help in making an application, and there was no assurance that I would get the approval. It was more likely that the CTC would consider it sufficient to have one air carrier serve what they perceived as a backwater. With these problems in mind, I flew over to Sullivan Bay.

The old place had changed hands four times since 1945, when Myrtle and Bruce Collinson had opened it up as a fuelling depot for boats and aircraft. The most recent takeover had just

occurred: my old friend Ursul Fox had sold the camp to a young American couple, Lynn and Mike Whitehead. Stopping in for fuel every day had brought me into contact with the new owners as soon as they moved into Sullivan's historic buildings. It was plain that the move had been Mike's idea; he was impatient to bring the twentieth century to Sullivan's electrical and plumbing systems and keen to get his new Cessna 180 seaplane from the States. Lynn, in contrast, appeared a little lost in her new wilderness home. It would be a safe guess that, during her early days in these north woods, she was missing the amenities of life in her home town of Seattle.

When I arrived that afternoon, the couple were nowhere to be seen. I fuelled BIU, then walked down the dock, checking the warehouse, the store and each bunkhouse in search of the owners. While I was approaching the lodge, an unusual sound assailed my ears—a high-pitched whine coming from the one-time loggers' bunkhouse. Throwing open the door, I was greeted by a cloud of sawdust, picked up by the breeze and blown around the room. Mike, who was operating a big electric sander, yelled at me to come in and shut the door. He had just about completed sanding the entire floor of what was to be the new lodge. The old

BIU preparing for takeoff out of Shawl Bay. Upon returning later that night, the bay was pitch black. Descending in a nose-high attitude and "feeling" for the water, I dropped it in from about four feet, knocking my passenger's hat off and jolting his unlit cigarette from his mouth.

varnish and years of imprints from a thousand caulked boots had all but disappeared, and the planks were showing through white.

"It's not really pristine," laughed Lynn, "but it's going to look a whole lot better." It was clear that the young couple had visions of trophy-covered walls, a crackling fire in the "airtight" stove and a warm sense of hospitality being enjoyed by tourists, boaters and sportfishermen. "So, young fellow," said Mike, "what's the drill?"

"Well, it's like this," I said, and gave them a brief rundown of the calamities on my plate, to which Mike responded with enthusiasm: "We'd love to have you operate from here. There's accommodation, you can set up your communication system here, Lynn can handle your dispatch—it will just be great. Sullivan is the right place for an airline."

I could have guessed that Mike

would be enthusiastic; he loved airplanes, and his comments were astute: the lodge would benefit from having a transportation system based right here. "In the meantime," he added, "here's our plan," and he began to outline in detail the couple's plans for Sullivan Bay. They would completely refurbish the place and turn it into a sportfishing camp, replank the docks, enlarge the store, install the electrical works, add a bigger generator and replumb the water and waste systems. "We're going to apply for a liquor store permit as well," exclaimed the enthusiastic Mike Whitehead.

The couple's vision would one day become a reality, but not as soon as was being planned. Fate had yet to play a trump card at the new Sullivan Bay Lodge.

5

BIU – LOGGERS AND OTHER HOOD ORNAMENTS

Returning from Minstrel Island one day, I began a gradual letdown through Pomfreys Pass. My usual procedure was to skim the seven-hundred-foot hill forming the west shoreline of Shawl Bay and then descend, by way of a 180-degree turn, back into the bay for the landing. BIU was halfway through the turn when, suddenly, a squawking sound arose from under the passenger seat beside me. It came from the citizens' band transceiver I had installed. This radio was illegal because aircraft are supposed to carry only aircraft-band VHF transmitters. The civil aviation authorities who make these rules have never flown a seaplane on the coast and are hard-pressed to figure out why an airplane needs a ship's radio. For their part, the seaplane operators point out that there are no towers out in the boonies, and for safety's sake seaplanes need to talk to the marine traffic in the inlets. The call I was receiving on the CB was about to prove that point.

"Jack, it's George. I'm hurt. Come and get me—quick." This time I heard the message clearly, and it was followed by a much stronger transmission from Edna Brown at Shawl Bay, now just off my right wing tip. "BIU, did you hear that?" she asked with obvious concern. I replied, "I've got it, Edna. Hang on, George, I'm on my way. I'll be there in three."

This had to be the flukiest message. The CB in the plane was normally a dead loss because the assigned frequencies for this system were so cluttered with boat traffic that the chance of getting a message through was most unlikely. Now, here was George Mooney, a handlogger working in Wakeman Sound, raising me with an emergency message that he needed help. I stuffed the Cessna's nose down and traded altitude for knots, banking around the corner of Wakeman Sound and flaring onto the water in front of George's beach camp in less than the

Facing page: The author, looking rather grim, around the time of the incident described in this chapter. This photo was taken by writer/photographer Ulli Steltzer, who at the time was researching her wonderful photo-narrative *Coast of Many Faces.* (This was one of the faces she understandably didn't use in her book.) Ulli and her co-author, Catherine Kerr, cadged rides in and out of the villages in exchange for my future use of her outstanding photography.

promised three minutes. I knew the depth of water here from previous calls at this same tide, so I landed close to the beach, turned away from shore into the wind, then hauled up the water rudders to fade back onto the pebbly shore. As I poled myself to the beach with the paddle handle, I could hear the brush cracking nearby. George burst into the clearing, clutching his leg above the knee. He hobbled as fast as he could toward the plane.

"Get back in and fire it up, Jack. Get me to Alert Bay hospital!" he yelled at me. He was making it up the struts into the passenger seat as I cranked her over. We took off straight out of the beach and hung a full-rate turn out of the bay with the wing tip's reflection in the water showing a bare six inches of separation. "If I pass out, just keep going," George said, still clutching his coveralls, where torn flesh and blood were in great evidence. He was leaking blood onto the cockpit floor as he fished a cigarette out of his pack with one hand and lit it without letting go of the oozing wound in his leg.

I called Edna to ask her to call Alert Bay, but being on the ball, she had already set up an ambulance to meet me. "They want you at the boat dock right in front of the hospital. They don't have an ambulance available," she advised. I answered in the affirmative, but I knew

this would pose a problem because there were pilings all along that dock and no way to lay a seaplane alongside without crumpling six feet off my wing. Maybe across the end, I thought, so long as there isn't a boat there.

George Mooney had been up in the bush working on his own. This was not a recommended method of logging, but it was common for handloggers who jump their trees out of their shoreline claims by using a long line tied to a powerful boat. George's injuries were a result of the chainsaw "climbing up his leg," also a common occurrence in the bush. A branch or loose brush can deflect the chain suddenly and catch even an experienced man like George unawares. The damage is ghastly, with the whirling chain pulling flesh out of the wound and leaving a wide, jagged slash and resulting in a profuse loss of blood.

George was into his second smoke when we touched down at Alert Bay, coming off the step in front of the boat dock. There was one space available near the end of the dock. No one was there to catch my wing tip, so I had to invent a solution to miss the pilings. I came alongside the dock with my wing tip just splitting the middle of the walkway, leaving about two feet of room between the wing tip and the pilings. Wind and tidal back eddies wanted to turn me out, so I helped them and kicked

on full right rudder while cutting the engine. The aircraft swung out and the tail started its journey across the dock, heading for those ugly creosoted pilings.

I went down the step in one movement onto the rear of the float and vaulted to the wharf from the heel of the pontoon. I raced aft and caught the tail plane before it pushed me into the water or crunched on a piling. Quickly, walking the plane backward, I slid the wing between two pilings before tying off my shore line. Docking under such conditions terrified me—the thought of damaging an aircraft while docking is a constant threat. Although most pilots will fly anywhere in most weather conditions without a tremor, docking at some of the places they're required to go truly tests their mettle.

George was picked up out of the passenger seat by a burly male nurse, who then carried him up the ramp and off to St. George's Hospital, where Doc Pickup waited. This human ambulance service explained why they wanted me to dock so close to the emergency ward. But George Mooney was a tough little man, and once he was stitched up he wouldn't take Doc Pickup's advice to stay in the hospital overnight. He hobbled out of the operating room and barked at me, "C'mon Jack, we're going home." We immediately flew back to Shawl Bay, where George had stored his

speedboat. He got aboard and waved goodbye to everybody on the dock, planning to be at his home in Halfmoon Bay, near Sechelt, later that night.

"That little bugger'll probably stop at Minstrel for a beer," laughed Alan Brown. We all watched in amazement as George's boat turned out of the bay, leaving behind a blue cloud of exhaust. George never came back to Shawl Bay during my time there, and I never saw him again.

What kind of men would choose to live alone up here and shake a living out of this country? It took a tough guy to survive the bush. There were characters who appeared as if from nowhere and often returned the same way they came, whereas others came to stay and made a name for themselves. Most were loggers, at one time or other, but were forced by circumstances or advancing years to work at anything available, such as watching camp for the logging companies or guiding for sport fishermen. Of all the characters I flew, none could hold a candle to Jerry Major.

He came down the path like a bullet; long strides at the full run, jumping from the bank to the rocky beach and scrambling to the seaplane dock as I cut the power and glided toward the float at Jennis Bay. I was half out the door, reaching for the painter when he exploded onto the dock, grabbed the

42

lift strut and walked the plane to a stop by pulling it against the dock fenders.

"Figured I could make it. Heard you coming over Bugaboo Lake. That's how they all come when the wind's blowing westerly—Jerry Major," he said, stuffing his hand into mine. It was then that I first noticed how long his legs and arms were—"gangly" would be the best description for him, but he was obviously nimble and well coordinated. "C'mon up to the house. Don't expect a mansion, though. I'm still working on it." He started off down the dock at a helluva clip, and I had trouble keeping pace with him. "You're that flying salesman guy. Selling electronic stuff. I gotta problem—bet you can fix me up." So much for introductions.

When we got to the house I had to agree with Jerry Major—it was no mansion. The house had last been the living quarters for Weldwood's superintendent at least two years earlier and had been left open for two heavy winters. It was now hardly livable. Jerry Major thought it was a great place and described how he was going to move this wall over here, punch a big bay window in right there, insulate the place and put a big fireplace on that wall. "Fieldstones," he said "I like fieldstone fireplaces. People in town would pay a million bucks for that view."

He rustled through some boxes and came up with a portable TV set, which

he wagged at me. "This set can't pick up a signal around here. It's this stupid thing." He pointed to the little pull-up antenna. "I need a really good Yagi." He was on the move again, beckoning me to follow him out of the house and up the road. We did a couple of city blocks in marathon time and arrived, puffing, at a large steel building that had been the logging company's garage, where they had repaired heavy equipment. It was a good building of corrugated steel, with two bays each capable of holding a logging truck or a Caterpillar tractor. The roof peak was about sixty feet from the ground, and my amiable customer had earlier taken his TV set up to the peak and determined that there was a signal to be had. He wanted the best possible antenna I could supply with a twenty-foot pipe, a roof jack and all the guy wires and insulators required.

Jerry Major had a good grasp of the subject and described to me an all-wave antenna system with remote power control so that he could rotate the head and fine-tune the signal from down in the house. I was impressed with his knowledge and flew away with his order in my pocket. It was an official order written on a stock-order pad and rubber-stamped in the name of "Major Enterprises."

"Have you met the new fellow up at

Jennis?" I asked Ursul Fox as he pumped gas into my 172 at Sullivan Bay. Ursul grunted, and I could tell he was not impressed. He was standing on a three-step stepladder, and when he finished filling my tank he came down and looked me in the eye. "If I were you, I would get cash for anything he buys. He's crazier than a fart." With those unkind words to consider, I turned out from the dock at Sullivan and continued the return leg of my monthly sales trip. I would be returning next month with Jerry's antenna strapped onto the floats of the Cessna if his company cheque, rubber-stamped like the order, didn't bounce.

"You take the pipe and the roof jack. I'll take everything else." Jerry Major was gone before I could explain that I couldn't stand heights and that I only sold the stuff, I didn't do installations. But he was gone up the steel ladder that was bolted to the back of the corrugated building. Like a jackrabbit, he was up on the roof, striding around as if he was out for an evening stroll rather than sixty feet off the ground on a steep, slippery steel roof.

I gripped the antenna pipe and stuffed the bag of parts under my shirt, starting up the ladder with great reluctance. I was so terrified of heights that I'd probably freeze rigid if I ever got up

there. I told Jerry this as I reached the eaves, but he just laughed, not taking my comment seriously—I was, after all, a pilot. When I crossed over onto the second ladder that was bolted to the roof, my knees started to knock and I was holding on to the ladder so hard my fist ached. I made it to the top and straddled the peak, breathing very deeply and not looking down. I told myself that courage is doing something you don't want to do. By those terms, I was a candidate for the Victoria Cross.

"Come over here into the middle and fasten the roof jack," Jerry said while ambling carelessly down to the edge of the roof, where he screwed in an eye-bolt, into which he strung some guy wires. Without looking down I worked my way to the location he had indicated and somehow fastened the roof jack. Jerry mounted the twenty feet of pipe with the antenna on top and did everything else in no time flat. I held on, straddling the roof in a seated position, trying not to look terrified. When he was finished, Jerry strolled down to the eavestrough and stepped, hands free, onto the top rung of the ladder. "I'm going to watch TV down at the house," he said. "Are you going to join me?" I was thankful that he did not stay to see me inch my way down the two ladders to the ground.

Back in the house, Jerry fiddled with

the power control and adjusted the fine tuning on what turned out to be a pretty marginal signal. He finally got Channel 2, but there was plenty of snow on the little black-and-white screen. I was glad I had cashed his cheque and that it hadn't bounced.

While Jerry fiddled with the TV set I was drinking, with some reluctance, from a cup he had cleaned with his shirt cuff and filled with the battery acid he called coffee. Pinned on the wall beside me was a large torn and yellowing photograph of a man standing atop a towering fir tree. The top of the tree had been cut off and was on its way to the ground. The man was standing on one foot on the topmost six-inch stub of the main trunk and was posturing for all the world like a ballet dancer or the hood ornament on a Rolls-Royce. The fearless balancer was easily identified as my friend, Jerry Major. "Yeah, I'm a high rigger by trade," he admitted.

Later, when we started the airline out of Shawl Bay, Jerry was one of the first to call for a load of groceries to be flown in to him at Jennis Bay. We renewed our acquaintance as we off-loaded the grub. Although I declined his offer of coffee, I did walk up the road with him to a little shack he had built on the shore of Huaskin Lake. Here, he described what he had been telling me about all the way up from the dock:

his million-dollar scheme.

"There has been a gold mine floating around in this lake since 1930," he exclaimed, referring to millions of board feet of cedar logs that had been cut down and discarded into the lake during the early exploitation of this logging site. "Those early loggers didn't want cedar," Jerry explained. "They wanted the fir, and to get at it they cut down hundreds of cedar trees and just threw 'em into the lake." He went on to explain that this area of the coast produced the finest cedar in the world and was well known by all the shake manufacturers in that industry for its quality of wood. He was going to split shakes from all those logs in the lake, and since he didn't have to fell the trees and drag them out to his shake mill, he would make a larger profit than anyone else because he would employ only himself and one other shake cutter. "When I need more logs, the westerly wind just blows them up on the beach," he exclaimed with his usual enthusiasm.

Taking me into the shack, Jerry showed me what he had been doing here at Jennis all these months. In the shack were several huge stacks of split shakes. He pulled a shake out of the pile and handed it to me. "The finest shakes in the world from Huaskin Lake," he said proudly. As shakes go, I had to admit it was a beauty.

45

Huaskin Lake is roughly E-shaped and has over ninety miles of shoreline. Jerry's description of the number of cedar logs in the water was quite correct, for the lake is choked with the silvery, weathered timber that shifts from one end of the lake to the other as the wind swings from southeast to westerly. "The natural oil of the cedar has protected this wood for the last forty years," grinned my ambling high rigger. "I sure owe a debt of gratitude to those old loggers."

Over the next year, I flew supplies into Jerry's camp at Jennis Bay and occasionally took the enthusiastic shake cutter over to Port Hardy or Port McNeill. He always paid me by company cheque, and the cheques were always good. His house never changed and the fieldstone fireplace never materialized, but the man worked night and day splitting shakes. He hired other shake cutters from time to time, but none of them lasted too long because the amenities at Jennis Bay were somewhat lacking unless you had a vision like Jerry's.

Jerry, who hailed from Kellogg, Idaho, became well known among the few who populated these parts. Many figured him to be mildly crazy, while others figured he was "on something." He would arrive in Sullivan Bay driving the strangest boat—a six-foot-square wooden box, whose sides or gunwales (if one offered the device boat status)

measured about eighteen inches high. Jerry had mounted an outboard on one end and would drive it, balls to the wall, from a standing position. The thing would plane at about a forty-five-degree angle and do about twenty knots on a slow day. Jerry would arrive at Sullivan Bay in this thing and pick up his mail or buy a few supplies, using the trip as an excuse to visit and tell a few war stories. On one occasion, while heading home out of Sullivan, he hit a rock close to shore and holed "the box" up near the bow. Although it took on water, he found that by increasing power he could hold the bow high and she wouldn't ship water. He never patched the hole. Instead, he just drove it hard and stood a little further aft. "It'll be fine unless the motor quits," he laughed.

The man's enthusiasm spilled into other fields of endeavour. In his spare time Jerry was writing a book, which he had begun many years earlier in Idaho. He gave me the book to take back to Shawl Bay to read. It was eleven inches thick, contained thousands of double-spaced, typewritten pages and was bound between two pieces of 8" by 11" quarter-inch plywood. He explained that it was a saga, commencing with a sort of biography of a wise old man he had known in Kellogg. I thought his writing was excellent, but although each paragraph had meaning in itself, it didn't join with the next to go anywhere. I read bits and pieces throughout the book and could make no sense of it at all. It was as if Jerry had jotted down every thought that had ever entered his head but didn't have a plan for where it was all going.

One day I received a call from Jerry on the radio phone, asking to charter the plane down to Vancouver the next day. It would be a long flight and pretty costly, so I warned him of the cost. He assured me that he knew what he was doing and that money was no object: "Man, I have hit pay dirt."

When I landed at Jennis Bay early the next morning, Jerry was waiting for me on the dock. It was not the Jerry Major I knew. This was the businessman, Gerald Major, for he was spiffed up—he was going to town. As he climbed into the plane the smell of Brut aftershave hit me like the perfume in a whore's boudoir, and I had to grin at my passenger. Jerry's sports jacket was a tad short in the arms and his pants were equally short in the legs, but he was wearing startlingly white socks, which filled in the space between his pant cuffs and his gleaming oxfords. The entrepreneur of Jennis Bay was going to town.

We tied up at the Bayshore Inn in downtown Vancouver, and Jerry took a cab to some lawyer's office on Pender Street. I waited at the Bayshore over endless coffees. Jerry arrived back around four o'clock, and I knew we would have to race against the sun to get back to Jennis Bay before dark. My main concern was the fear of arriving at Jennis Bay too late to get home to my snug barge at Shawl Bay. The thought of a night in Jerry's mansion drove me to carry a little more manifold pressure than recommended by the manufacturer, but we still didn't make it. I had to land at Shawl Bay and invite Jerry to sleep over. He spotted his book on my table and proceeded to read it to me.

He never did go to bed, and his voice droned on into the night. The next morning, while I was totally wiped from lack of sleep, Alan Brown doubled up with laughter when I told him about my experience. Alan figured Jerry was about the funniest guy on the coast. From that day on, he never failed to chuckle over my drawing the short straw and getting Jerry Major as a roommate.

When in Vancouver, Jerry had signed a contract with a Whonnock-based shake company that was prepared to take an initial order of two barge-loads of Huaskin shakes for delivery to the States. As Jerry had stated, he had hit pay dirt. It looked like Jerry Major was going to have the last laugh on those who derided him. He went back to work with a vengeance.

I didn't see much of Jerry for several

months. Then, one lovely fall afternoon, I was coming out of Sullivan Bay, banking into Wells Channel en route to Port Hardy, when I spotted a tug beneath me, near the mouth of the inlet. The ship had two huge barges in tow, each stacked high with the most beautiful shakes in the world. A sensation of great joy swept over me, and I cheered aloud for Jerry's success. This eccentric man who had been the butt of many jokes and derisive remarks was going to walk out of this country with dollars in his pocket—no mean feat for anyone.

I cannot recall how many months went by before I received a call from Jennis Bay, ordering a plane to Port Hardy. When I arrived, Jerry was decked in his going-to-town gear, complete with Brut. I dropped him in Port Hardy, where he rebooked me to come back in two days, at which time he would have a couple of additional passengers. "My family are coming to visit for the summer," he said. I was floored, as was everyone on the mid-coast. No one had known that Jerry Major had a family.

When Jerry's family arrived, this amazing event was compounded by the revelation that "the family" totalled one wife and eleven kids. The coastal radio phones were abuzz, as was Jennis Bay with this invasion of children ranging from toddlers to a seventeen-year-old.

Jerry hadn't been home to Idaho for at least two years, so people were checking out ages and counting on their fingers until it was revealed that some of the younger kids had been adopted.

During the two months of the family visit, Jerry appeared very content. He looked well fed, bathed and cleanly dressed, with regular haircuts. He would appear with the group at Sullivan Bay on Sundays in a holiday spirit. Lynn Whitehead hired one of Jerry's daughters, the seventeen-year-old, for chambermaid duties at Sullivan Bay, and she and my son Peter, who was also helping out around the place, fell madly in love for that summer. When the family left at summer's end, Peter went home with his first broken heart and Jerry Major returned to Jennis Bay a more respected man of the community, now projecting prosperity and stability.

Jerry's prosperous period ended very abruptly. When those Huaskin shakes found their way onto the roofs of homes in the States, the intense heat and sunlight dried the last vestige of Huaskin Lake out of the wood. The natural cedar oil, which was presumed to have preserved the shakes during forty years of immersion in the lake, had in fact disappeared. The shakes split. What had been a beautiful shake roof, the pride of the California owner, became, in less than a month, just so much expensive

48

kindling. The broken shakes turned silver in the California sun, while Jerry Major's dreams turned to stone.

The lawsuits and countersuits rained on Jerry like the winter storms of Drury Inlet. His trips to Sullivan Bay were now more purposeful than those earlier, convivial family visits. Sullivan now had a liquor store, and the box boat appeared more regularly. The motor did quit on him one night, and Jerry had to take refuge on a reef in the middle of Drury Inlet. He spent the night on the rock, until the tide nudged him off and he had to swim for it. Jerry Major's luck wasn't running out—it was gone.

I flew into Jennis Bay one morning while passing on the way up the coast. Jerry was more than his old self. It wasn't just a bear that he had shot as it tried to enter his house (this had been one of his earlier stories), but a flying saucer that had landed in the garden. The craft, blazing with lights and with strange green men aboard, had decided that Jerry wouldn't be a proper specimen to take home to Uranus and had left before any witnesses could confirm that Jerry's UFO wasn't just a space ship in a bottle.

Stories from Jennis Bay abounded: there was the arrival of Consolidated Mining & Smelting to confirm with Jerry that he had found a gold claim in McKinnon Lagoon; later, the story developed that CM&S would soon commence developing the claim, and Jerry was again in the chips. But CM&S, like the green men, went home empty-handed. This major development was, in fact, a Major invention.

My flying days out of Shawl Bay and Sullivan Bay came to an end at about this time, and I took up a flying job with a road-building company out of Campbell River. My flights for this company, LTJ Contracting, often took me into my old stamping grounds and occasionally I would get into Shawl Bay for coffee with the Browns or into Sullivan Bay to keep up with the local gossip. News of Jerry Major thinned out, and I relegated him to that special recess of the brain labelled "people to write about."

In a journey logbook I kept in CF-ERQ, the construction company's 185, one entry states, "Jerry Major is gone." He had called for a pickup from Gulf Air's north coast scheduled flight. When the single Otter arrived, Jerry was found lying on the dock, decked out in his going-to-town clothes. He was in great pain and was rushed to hospital, but he never recovered from advanced liver cancer.

Whenever I think of this amazing man, I still see him posturing on one foot on that giant fir tree, his arms spread-eagled, looking for all the world like a ballet dancer or the hood ornament on a Rolls-Royce.

49

CRAZY EDDIE

The company was formed in 1977 by Edward Emery Carder. He called it "Minstrel Air," after the island he owned on British Columbia's mid-coast. It had been a long time coming, this licence to operate an air charter service, but the Canadian Transport Commission had ruled in favour of his application, and Ed Carder's latest business venture was launched. He immediately went out and bought himself a Cessna 180 seaplane and had the proud new name of "Minstrel Air" painted on the tail. It was this little red-and-white floatplane that would be a mute witness to the series of amazing events about to unfold at Minstrel Island.

When Ed Carder applied for his air carrier licence he revealed to the authorities that he was a landed immigrant in Canada, having come here from his home in Tacoma, Washington, immediately following the Vietnam war, in which he served as a helicopter pilot. He had also declared his occupation as that of "teacher." Indeed, he was the principal, teacher and janitor of the Minstrel Island rural school.
The school board at nearby Port Hardy deemed themselves very fortunate to have found someone with a master's degree in education out there in the boonies. The enterprising Ed Carder himself had established the need for a school at Minstrel Island by proving to the board that the required number of students resided in the area to warrant a facility right on his own little island.

In addition to teaching, Ed had refurbished the old cottages on Minstrel Island and rebuilt the system of docks. He installed fresh water and electrical outlets on the docks, installed fuel tanks on the high part of the island and commenced operation as a resort with a well-stocked general store and fuel-dispensing facilities for both marine and aviation gas. He took over the post office operation from a long-time local resident and obtained a licence to establish a liquor outlet, and now he had an airline! The sleepy old port of call for long-defunct Union Steamships was coming alive again.

52

Another side of Ed Carder's character revealed itself at this point: the school board found that the number of students in the Minstrel Island school had fallen below the required number and that Ed had failed to report this fact. It seems that when Ed heard that a school board official was coming over to Minstrel Island, he would "stock" his classroom with every young person he could find in the area; some of his counterfeit students would be picked up from visiting boats for such occasions. How many times he was able to get away with this is unknown, but eventually the school board got the picture, closed down the Minstrel Island school and fired Ed Carder from his thirty-thousand-dollar-a-year job. Ed remarked to me during these events that he had never minded getting his pay as a teacher, but his conscience had bothered him when he accepted the two hundred dollars a month paid to him for performing the janitorial services for the one-room school.

Before his dismissal by the Port Hardy school board, Ed applied to the government of Canada for an LIP grant. The letters stood for "Local Initiative Program," and local initiative was something Ed had a lot of. He convinced the federal authorities that the "community" of Minstrel Island required a community hall. If they would put up a mere thirty thousand dollars, he, Ed Carder, would build it and maintain it. With his application, Ed sent along numerous photographs depicting Minstrel Island as a busy little community. Not surprisingly, the feds took the bait and coughed up thirty grand. Ed had not passed on the information that his family of four were the entire "community" at Minstrel. He must have enjoyed building the hall, which in fact was used as a barn for his children's pet—a donkey.

With his wife and two young sons operating the resort and the busy store, Ed could now devote all his attention to developing his airline. He started to fly local charter flights to the Native villages of Kingcome and Gilford, providing those customers with a connection to nearby Alert Bay. Ed solicited the many logging camps in the area, and soon the little seaplane was flying loggers, Natives and fishermen in and out of camp and hauling groceries and supplies from Campbell River and Kelsey Bay. Seeing a growth potential, he purchased another plane, installed his own docks at Alert Bay and sent his eldest boy to Vancouver for flying lessons. A family airline was in the offing.

While Ed was roaring around the north coast in his little airplane, he was developing a reputation; he would fly anywhere, in any weather. After all, nobody was shooting at him as they had in Vietnam, so what was a little low visibility, storm-force winds and high seas? When his competitors were shut down because of the weather, Ed scooped all the business and laughed all the way to the bank. He got the name of "Crazy Eddie" and lived up to it in a series of hair-raising flights that started with a near thing at Campbell River. Ed ran out of gas a few miles short of the seaplane base. Forced to "deadstick" into the log-booming grounds at Menzies Bay, Ed called nearby Island Airlines on the radio on his way down: "Send a boat to pick up my three passengers, and send over ten gallons of gas!" Ed's plea for help was overheard by a visiting Transport Canada inspector, who himself delivered the gas—along with a suspension to Ed's operating certificate for dangerous flying.

The next "incident" was funny to all except the United Church flying preacher, Don Isner, who made Ed Carder's acquaintance the hard way. Taxiing his church-owned aircraft to position for takeoff on the busy mouth of the Campbell River, the preacher watched in horror as a landing plane flared for touchdown directly in his path. Powerless to get out of the way in time, the preacher did what he knew best—he prayed.

In Ed Carder's airplane (for, indeed, it was the intrepid aviator himself) the passenger screamed a warning to the preoccupied pilot, "Look out!" Ed firewalled the throttle and yanked the aircraft off the water. The plane, desperately short of airspeed, staggered into the air, its snarling propeller sawing past the preacher's head so closely that he could read the serial number. For a second it looked like they would make it, but the spreader bar between the pontoons of Ed's plane connected with the preacher's tail and ripped it off, as Ed's Cessna staggered through the air, desperately clawing for altitude to clear the buildings on the adjacent spit.

The preacher, undoubtedly in a hurry to reach the closest laundromat, taxied back to the dock, dragging his tail behind him, so to speak. Ed came back for a less eventful landing and joined his "victim" at the dock, where arrangements were made for the repair of the church aircraft. "I have a wedding to perform in Port McNeill in an hour," complained the shaken minister. "No problem," said Ed, "I'll fly you up there," which he did, and promptly charged the church for the charter. And he never paid for the repairs to the church plane.

It would be safe to say that Ed's preoccupation with his many businesses and his attempt to do too much each day were the main causes of his rash of mishaps. The logbook entries for his new Cessna, CF-SOX, show that on one particular day he performed thirty-six charters. Returning home to Minstrel Island long after dark that night, he landed crosswind on the water in front of the resort and flipped his shiny new plane into the ocean. On another occasion, when scooping the day's business from his more conservative competitors, Ed landed in sixty-knot gusts and found himself swimming for the beach.

These escapades did little to deter the public from flying with Minstrel Air. It is well known that a logger wanting to get out of camp will fly with anyone. Freight and drunks never ask for a pilot's licence, and it's amazing just how much can be covered up or escape public notice despite the efficiency of the legendary "moccasin telegraph" in this area. Minstrel Air continued to thrive.

Ed hired an additional pilot, David Reaville, and his two little red-and-white seaplanes were seen everywhere. With his wife, Margit, performing the dispatch duties out of Minstrel Island and another office in operation in Alert Bay, things were looking better than ever. Down at Kelsey Bay, long-time residents Bill and Gert Kelly were doing an excellent job of looking after Ed's interests, so a few mishaps could be handled.

In Campbell River the "big guys," Gulf Air and Island Air, were taking notice of this upstart with more than casual interest. Another entrepreneur by the name of Jimmy Pattison would soon have their full attention, buying them out, forming Air BC and leaving Ed Carder to his own devices. About this time, Ed Carder's devices started to run out.

One Sunday morning, the radio phone at Minstrel Island resort announced a call for Minstrel Air. A logger at Shoal Harbour wanted a bottle of scotch. He wanted it bad enough to pay for the charter of Ed's plane from Minstrel to Shoal Harbour and back—not an unusual request from a thirsty logger on the weekend, but when Ed arrived on the dock with the bottle it was not a logger who greeted him, but an inspector from the liquor control board. Somebody out there didn't like Ed, and they got him where it hurt. The liquor control board shut down the liquor store at Minstrel Island.

Not long after this setback, another disaster befell Ed Carder's enterprise: the store at Minstrel Island burned to the ground, and hard on the heels of this event, the fire marshal condemned the fuel-dispensing system at the resort. Ed's empire was falling apart, and it seemed that as fast as he tried to repair it, something else would happen. The next occurrence was bizarre in the extreme: Ed was charged with two counts of sexual assault. This staggering revelation had first been reported in a newspaper account of a coastal pilot who had confronted a woman resident on a floatcamp and, finding her alone, had assaulted her after a prolonged chase along the dock and in and out of several small boats. Hardly had this amazing report come to light than another charge of a similar nature was laid against the pilot by a woman resident of Minstrel Island, who claimed that Ed shut off the island's power plant and then assaulted her in her lonely, darkened cabin in a heavily treed area of the island.

Following these revelations came the cruellest cut of all. Ed's wife, Margit, was reported to be terminally ill with brain cancer and was not expected to live past Christmas.

Early one October morning, Ed Carder landed his seaplane at Port McNeill and discharged his passenger, Dr. John Fitzgerald, at the town seaplane dock. Ed knew John Fitzgerald well because he had flown him regularly on the doctor's rounds of the Native villages on the mainland. On the way over from Scott Cove this particular morning, they had flown past a pod of whales and Ed, quite out of character for this usually businesslike pilot, swooped down and circled the playful orcas before continuing across the straits to his destination. Waving goodbye to Fitzgerald, Ed pushed away from the dock and took off past the breakwater and over Ledge Point, bound for his next stop at Knight Inlet. It was the last time anyone ever saw Ed Carder. A massive air search failed to find the familiar aircraft, and after nine days Ed Carder joined the legion of the missing and was presumed dead. Margit Carder died a few months later.

I am chief pilot for the new owner of Minstrel Air. I sit here in Minstrel Island, in Ed Carder's chair, and look out, through his window, at the scene he knew so well: a complex of docks and buildings that make up the old Union Steamships port of call. Behind me, the hotel leans into the hill, as it has done since 1904. The electrical system Ed installed on the docks hangs limp from the pole line. A single yacht attempts to use the water line, but the meter Ed installed is no longer operating and the light plant is cold. The yacht moves on. Ed's airplane is mine now. It tugs at its moorings on the float that this energetic man had built for it—this is the new plane that he had liked so much and had sunk twice. The old plane, CF-ZSZ, went with him, wherever he is. The charred stumps of the pilings that once supported his store are mute testimony to the once-feverish activity of this place. A gay little sign, painted by two young boys, squeaks in the constant breeze—it describes the joys of flying to Mount Waddington by Minstrel Air. It entices no one.

A sea bird drops a shell—a brief flash in the sun—the splash and the ripple are lost in the greater movement of the sea.

INTERLUDE: CRAZY EDDIE

When Ed Carder disappeared, many claimed that he had simply skipped out of a life that was doomed to tragedy. Faced with the criminal charges against him and the impending death of his wife, Ed was considered, by the supporters of this theory, to be capable of such an act. These people believed Ed to be alive somewhere, in hiding. "He'll show up some day," they would claim, or "Maybe he won't, but Ed's alive and well—somewhere."

I didn't subscribe to this theory; I had been flying on the day that Ed had disappeared, and I knew how the fog had been hanging in the inlets that morning. I figured Ed had "bought the farm" by trying to get through the fog to Kingcome or Knight Inlet, or by flying "on top" and getting caught above cloud or between layers, unable to find a hole through which to descend.

Several times in the following years, I would hear a rumour that Ed had been spotted in Toronto or on the beach in Hawaii. Once, when I was flying alone in silence, a voice over the radio cried, "Ed Carder's been spotted! They found his plane in the States somewhere!" This voice, which had just come out of the blue, never identified itself. I laughed, believing that someone enjoyed perpetuating the rumour.

On October 1, 1989, I boarded a Canadian Airlines flight out of Edmonton to Fort St. John. Halfway into the one-hour flight, I laid down my newspaper and looked around the crowded cabin at my fellow travellers. My eyes strayed to the seat one row ahead of me, on the opposite side. It was a familiar-looking back of the head, and the bearded profile of this passenger created a nagging sense of recognition in my mind. Somewhere, I had talked with this man—on docks, I thought. Had I sold him radio equipment in his general store, attended a school board social function with this man and danced with his attractive young wife? Had I been at one time a friend and later a competitor, and for many years just a fellow pilot? Had I not lived in this man's house, where many of his belongings had been abandoned, including a portrait of him and his wife on the mantelpiece? Had I not flown this man's airplane, and had I not made the next entry in the logbook under his own last signature, back when I had flown for the new Minstrel Air after his disappearance? Ed Carder was now, if my memory was not playing tricks, sitting across the aisle from me as the jet prepared to land at Fort St. John.

I did not speak to him. What do you say to a dead man? I got off to change planes while he stayed on and continued the flight to either Fort Nelson or Watson Lake. I did make official inquiries.

Many months later I was told that the man I fingered as the deceased Ed Carder was someone else from Labrador, and I guess he just looked like Ed—from the back, from the side, from the front. I suppose that when our eyes locked and he turned away, furtively, it was my imagination. That's how the authorities explained it, anyway. They also admitted that the case file on Ed Carder remains open.

One day, during my Minstrel Island stint, when I was living in Ed's house and flying his airplane, I was busying myself on the seaplane dock, cleaning up the plane, readying it for a day of flying. I was in need of a length of electrician's tape and was desperately searching the little oil-and-supplies shack that Ed had built on the seaplane dock. There was no tape to be found among the cans of engine oil, window cleaner and paper towels stored in that little building, so I turned to Ed's duffle coat, which was hanging on the door. Surely that efficient pilot would have kept a roll of the stuff somewhere, I thought, as I stuffed my hand into one of the coat pockets.

To my delight and amazement my hand closed around the familiar shape of a roll of the very tape I was seeking. Before closing the shed door, I thought to check Ed's other coat pocket, for I had often seen him wearing this coat, and the little things as may be found in a man's pocket are most revealing. Such was my motive, for the sensation of having found the tape was disquieting—I had touched this man's personal life for an instant. I withdrew from Ed's other pocket a handful of condoms.

If the charges against Ed Carder were true, he assaulted two women and escaped from the law. Whatever the reality, Ed did not escape the tragedy of his own life.

6

BMO – Lost and Found

Following the sale of the airline, I was faced with finding another plane to replace BIU. Bill Fouty was anxious to get his plane back, and I was becoming desperate to the point of considering shutting down the whole operation. The added pressure of Ed Carder's Minstrel Air flying into what I had deemed to be my own private territory was taking its toll, and I despaired that all my past hard work was for nought.

Could I expect to receive another phone call that would solve all my business problems? Not a chance, you say? Well, this is the aviation business, and something always happens. A significant phone call did come from an otherwise sane person, one who was smitten with the desire to put airplanes to work, and off I went again, back to Shawl Bay to pick up where I had left off.

I returned with a new airplane, an immaculate orange-and-white Cessna 185 bearing the ident of CF-BMO. Responding to the Brown family's interest in BMO, now tied up to the seaplane dock, I explained that a prominent doctor from Port Hardy had engaged me as a partner in a project to establish an airline under the name of Vancouver Island Air. Dr. Vern Kemp, a physician in Port Hardy, was pursuing the acquisition of a licence under this name, but in the meantime we would continue to fly under the Aquila licence, now owned by Qualicum Beach resident John Molliett.

"You've got horseshoes up your ass," said Alan Brown, amazed that we had survived this crisis.

We resumed our air operations, and in a few weeks it was business as usual. BMO performed flawlessly throughout the busy month of April and on into what became one of the hottest summers ever recorded on the mid-coast.

Down on Minstrel Island, Ed Carder was still waiting for his licence, and as the months passed we began to believe that we had as good a chance as he and that Vern's application might very well succeed.

On the morning of June 4, a Sunday, I slept in until nine o'clock and was invited to have breakfast with the Browns, who were all gathered in the kitchen nook. During the meal, Alan revealed that a call had come in from what he thought was Transport Canada, in Port Hardy. The signal had been very distorted, but he had caught something about Lynn Whitehead at Sullivan Bay. I thought about this for a few moments, wondering why Lynn would call me.

"I'm going to fly up to Sullivan," I announced after breakfast. "Maybe Lynn needs a plane." Cheryl Brown walked down to the aircraft with me and turned me out from the dock. Lynn and Mike Whitehead, the new owners of Sullivan Bay, had just brought in Mike's seaplane from Seattle—a Cessna 180 with the new Canadian registration SBL, standing for Sullivan Bay Lodge. The plane had been completely refurbished in Vancouver and was Mike's pride and joy. He was now flying guests around and performing regular flights to Campbell River for provisioning the lodge. Like all recently licensed pilots, Mike was looking for reasons to fly his new plane.

The seven miles up Sutlej Channel didn't take me long that warm Sunday

morning, and when I banked around the point and touched down on the calm water, Lynn was standing on the seaplane dock waiting for me. As I came alongside she grabbed the lift strut and held me onto the rubber tires on the dock. She looked pale and tense. I knew before she spoke that it was something to do with Mike and the plane.

"Mike's overdue from a flight up to Piper Lake," she stated. She started to turn me out from the dock. "Please fly up there and find out if he's still at the lake. It's been four hours since he and his three passengers left." I took off out of Sullivan, pointing the nose onto the direct route to the head of Smith Sound, where Piper Lake was located. This would have been Mike's route. If he had problems on the way up, there were plenty of lakes and waterways he could land on, and if he got onto Piper Lake and for some reason couldn't get off again, I would soon spot the bright-orange Cessna.

Scanning the terrain as I proceeded up to the lake, I arrived over Piper and found no sign of the plane. The water in the lake was very high, and the usual gravel bar he would have planned to beach upon had disappeared in the high water conditions. There was no sign of Mike, and he would have been out of gas two hours ago. Not good.

On the return trip I flew the coastal route, just in case he had chosen that way. I stopped at two logging camps and asked if they had heard a plane that morning. Since it was Sunday, the loggers had slept in and nobody had heard anything. I called Port Hardy tower, when closer in, advising them that SBL was not at its intended destination, and they agreed to pass on this information to search-and-rescue officials. Arriving back at Sullivan, I spotted a familiar Cessna tied to the dock. It belonged to Johnny Buck, a resort owner from Rivers Inlet. Buck's plane was secured behind an American 206. I slid in behind John's plane with just enough dock to tie up, and joined the gathering of glum people in the lodge.

"We've divided the area into three, Jack." Johnny tapped the map on the table with his pipe. "Mike has to be in one or other of these zones. I suggest we each search one of the zones for three hours and then return here for gas. We'll switch areas with each other and cover them again and again until we find him. He's got to be in there."

Each of the three aircraft took two spotters aboard and took off to comb the areas designated. After three hours, we had all drawn a blank. Night fell, and the impact of the distinct possibility that Mike had crashed descended upon us. I returned to Shawl Bay and discussed the situation with the Browns. Alan and Garry agreed to join me, as spotters, for the morning search.

Taking off from Sullivan before six o'clock the next morning, our plan was to use the cool, early hours to best advantage, but the day proved to be a scorcher right from the start. We tracked back and forth over the assigned area but found nothing. When we returned for gas, we swapped areas with Johnny Buck and searched the zone he had just completed while he reworked our area—all to no avail.

A person off the street is useless as a spotter. One must have some bush sense and a concept of what a plane down in the bush is likely to look like and what other types of evidence can provide a clue—one looks as much for a broken tree as for an airplane. We had one trained spotter in a prawn fisherman by the name of Vaughan Thompson. Vaughan had been in the U.S. air force and had been trained in aerial spotting. He passed on a few valuable hints to the rest of us before departing again with Johnny Buck.

We all returned that night, tired and discouraged, saddened by the growing certainty that Mike and his three passengers were in serious trouble. Also waiting for us was the news that the air force search-and-rescue squadron from

61

FLIGHTS OF A COAST DOG

Johnny Buck, with a planeload of groceries for his sport-fishing camp in Rivers Inlet. Johnny was flying the search aircraft that spotted the downed Cessna in Smokehouse Canyon after four days of intensive searching by three civilian aircraft and the search-and-rescue squadron from CFB Comox.

Comox had told Lynn to pull out those civilian search planes. Lynn told them to get stuffed. She pointed out that these civilians knew the country like the backs of their hands, knew what to expect of Mike and were more likely to find him than all those square searches now being performed by the air force out over the Pacific Ocean. The SAR people didn't like her decision, but they stayed on the search.

The missing aircraft had taken off with Mike flying Tom Coulter, a pilot and engineer visiting Sullivan with his girlfriend, Mandy Davis. Mike and Tom were going up to Piper Lake, where Tom would set up a camp for himself and Mandy. This accomplished, they were to fly back to Sullivan and pick her up. The couple planned to spend a few days fishing on Piper Lake before returning to their homes in Vancouver. Before takeoff, two men from a visiting yacht, the *Cobra*, asked if they could join Mike and Tom in the flight just to see the country. Mike was happy to have them aboard for the ride, and the four very large men took off in SBL.

On day four of the search, the certainty that we would find them all safe and sound had dissipated. We had run out of ideas, and each of the pilots returning from the first three-hour stint showed his discouragement. Lynn brought us all a heaping plate of sand-wiches and a large thermos of coffee, and we sat around the table in the lodge speculating on just where in hell that plane had gone. Mike Whitehead's family had arrived from Seattle, as had Lynn's parents, Ed and Hilda. The mood at Sullivan was one of despair.

Somebody said they had seen Mike carrying a camera to the plane, and Mandy stated that Tom also had one with him. He'd also taken binoculars, because he was an avid goat hunter and kept his eyes peeled for mountain goats when flying. It then came out that each of the guests had taken a camera.

"Goats," said Johnny Buck, himself a hunter. "I'll bet they were looking for goats." Somehow it was determined that more than one of the plane's occupants was a goat hunter. "If they went looking for goats, they'd be in higher country than where we've been looking. It would be up in here," he said, pointing out the area above Piper Lake—up in the Smokehouse Canyon area, where the terrain climbed as high as five thousand feet above sea level. Suddenly we were all charged with energy and keen to get going. It was a thin thread, but it was all we had to go on and gave us a renewed enthusiasm.

With only one spotter with me on this day, the search proved to be an even greater strain. Flying the plane in this more rugged, more demanding country while attempting to scan the steep slopes was very taxing. The stress of these last four days suddenly caught up with me near the end of the second three-hour search period. Exhausted and dazzled by the intense sunshine and heat, I slid the 185 into McKinnon Lagoon on the return flight to Sullivan. It had a derelict dock, and I tied there in the cool shade of the overhanging bank to regain myself. That stop provided the most welcome respite and made it possible to make it through the remainder of the day—a day that ended with the news that SBL had been found and that all her occupants were dead.

We flew back to Shawl Bay that evening, out of respect for the fact that Sullivan Bay was in shock. Lynn Whitehead, her parents, Mike's parents, Mandy Davis and the guests from the yacht *Cobra* could not believe the sinister chain of events that had occurred in such a beautiful, happy setting. The stunned survivors had only this evening to reconcile their grief, because the next morning, several yachts arrived at different times, each filled with holidaymakers in high spirits and totally ignorant of the tragedy into which they had sailed. Each demanded the services provided by this new boaters' spa and must have wondered why a pall of gloom prevailed. Near the end of that day, thirty-five construction workers also arrived to bunk in at Sullivan in preparation for the building of a fish ladder at nearby Embly Lagoon. Lynn was swept into action, preparing Sullivan for an onslaught of business at a time when she and the others were still reeling from the tragedy.

For those of us who still grieved for Mike, the atmosphere at Sullivan Bay for the remainder of the summer was a bizarre mixture of holiday spirit and tragedy, hijinks and deep gloom. At the end of August the construction workers left Sullivan Bay, their contract with the Department of Fisheries completed. Many of the pleasure boats also departed for home, and those who remained had motored down Sutlej Channel, homeward bound, before mid-September. There was a heavy dew on the floats in the mornings now, and the smoke from the lodge would hang among the trees in the still air.

The smell of fall was faintly perceptible. Though the days were clear, there was a crispness in the evening air as the activities at Sullivan Bay wound down. Doors and windows were closed in the late afternoon, and an occasional fire was lit in the "airtight" wood burner in the lodge. There was time now to ask a critical question, the answer to which would determine the future of Sullivan Bay. It was Lynn's dad, Ed Price, who turned to his daughter and rather reluctantly posed the question. "Are you going to stay on here, Lynn, or shut it down and come home with us to Seattle?"

Lynn had obviously had this question on her mind for many weeks. Her answer was quick: "I'm staying on, Dad. When Mike and I moved here, we had many plans for the place. I'm going to finish what we started." Ed took this news calmly, and then turned to me. "Would you consider moving your airline to Sullivan Bay for the winter, Jack? Lynn's going to need help and shouldn't be here on her own." I agreed out of hand, despite not knowing how it was going to work for the airline.

I flew Ed and Lynn's mom, Hilda, over to Port Hardy the next morning, where they boarded a plane for home. They told me of their plans to come up again next summer to help out around the place, and when they left their expressions could not conceal their many misgivings about their daughter's welfare over the long winter months ahead. Their plane was out of sight when I made my way to Hardy Bay, where BMO tugged at its moorings.

"Play 'Name that Song,' Jack." Lynn was draped over the easy chair next to the "airtight," and I leaned against what had been the bar but was now converted into the library, full of paperbacks. My trumpet came up and I blew about twelve bars of "Beale Street Blues," then modulated into "Don't Get Around Much Anymore," followed by half of "Stardust." I didn't complete any of the songs but would simply allow the last note of one to become the first note of the other. It was a nutty thing we were doing, but it was our only entertainment, and October and November are long months out here in the backwoods. As I played, Lynn would call out the names of the songs as she recognized them, and we would ultimately end up laughing and hitting the kitchen for grub. Clearly it was time to get out of here, before cabin fever drove us over the edge. We were also getting a little flak from some of the visiting pilots, who figured we were shacked up together. But we weathered these jibes and became fast friends.

The handlogger George Mooney had what we called the "hippie trailer," mounted on a raft of logs and stored at Shawl Bay. With George's blessings, we had towed it up to Sullivan Bay and cinched it to the dock next to the White House. I obtained a kerosene heater because the propane furnace in the trailer was not working. I moved in and secured the airplane to the main dock behind the trailer. The aircraft was now XRK, which Vern Kemp had recently purchased. He had taken back

65

BMO for his own use, and I was given this beautiful, factory-new airplane.

Each morning I would call Shawl Bay on the radio to get my charter trips and then fly off to service them. Communication at Sullivan was bad and we had a lot of trouble getting through, making it sometimes necessary to get in the air just to raise the Shawl Bay dispatch. This procedure went on for October and November, but as December arrived, so did a deep freeze that plunged us into clear, cold ten-below weather. The docks were coated with heavy frost, and in the mornings I would find the fuel frozen in the plane's fuel lines, which took several hours to thaw before I could get underway. A few days before Christmas, Lynn flew with me to Campbell River, where she took a flight to Seattle. I drove to my home in Qualicum Beach for the Christmas holidays.

Lynn had arranged for a mutual acquaintance to watch over our camp during our absence. Although she agonized over making this decision, getting away from "Name that Song" was just too appealing to resist. Following the Christmas holiday, Lynn arrived back at Sullivan Bay a few days before me. When I taxied up to the dock and jumped out of the plane, she was standing on the dock with a dubious look on her face. I knew

immediately something was wrong. I think I said something clever, like "What's up?"

Lynn gestured to the trailer. "Our friend's in your trailer." I was incredulous; this woman had agreed not to even open the door of the trailer while I was away. It was not mine to loan out. Lynn had made the lodge available for the camp watchers—there was no need to use any other facility. I was furious and pushed open the trailer door. The scene that greeted me was one of total devastation. Our "friend" was sitting on the bench seat, and two little kids in wet boots were running along the two top bunks. My bed clothing was all balled up and filthy. The wall in which the propane furnace was located was totally destroyed, and the whole of the trailer's interior was gutted by fire.

"We were very lucky, Jack," she said, explaining that they didn't have any water in the lodge, no heat: "Everything was frozen, Jack, so we had to move in here. Then the furnace caught fire, and we had to throw buckets of sea water on it to put it out. We were very luck, Jack."

I was furious and couldn't stand the horrible stink inside the trailer. I stormed out onto the dock, where Lynn was waiting with the next piece of news.

"Those two little darlings went from building to building, using the toilets, which were all filled with anti-freeze for the winter. They found the water taps and turned on the water, filling the pipes and hot-water tanks, which I had drained. The pipes froze and burst. The hot-water tanks froze and burst. There are six frozen and burst hot-water tanks, and several toilet bowls split from the ice. There was over three hundred gallons of stove oil in the tank when we left. There's not a drop left—you tell me." We both wanted to cry.

For the next week, Lynn and I disconnected hot-water tanks and threw them off the dock—all six of them. They are still there on the bottom, beneath Sullivan Bay. We installed new tanks as they arrived in Pat Finnerty's airplane and on the Gulf Air scheduled flight. It was a hell of a job, and I cannot remember finishing it before I conveniently flew off on a charter somewhere. To add to our problems, the power generator was giving us trouble, but out of the blue Pat arrived with a new and much larger generator and installed it for Lynn. Pat's appearances were more frequent after Christmas, and naive as I am, I started to realize that something was happening between these two. The trailer went back to Shawl Bay, and I bunked up in the second bedroom of the White House. On the first night in that bed, I threw back the sheets and crawled in wearing only my jockey shorts.

The sheets were so cold, having been without any heat in this room for months, that they were actually frozen. I leaped out of the bed in total shock and ran up the hall into Lynn's bedroom, which was the only heated room in the house. She was in her king-sized bed reading a book—the room was at about ninety degrees. To her amazement—and mine, later—I grabbed her extra eiderdown and curled up in the armchair at the foot of her bed. I think my words were something to the effect that social morality be damned. "I'm not sleeping in that room—you've got a roommate tonight." We both burst out laughing as she drew out a demarkation zone across the foot of her bed. "Cross it and you're dead," she laughed.

The next day, we put some heat into the other bedroom and got it thawed out. I slept there for a few nights but grew to hate the dog, Sully, who during the night would make a large deposit on the rug beside me, making any midnight tiptoeing to the biffy very treacherous and fouling the cold air. I was thinking he might "take a swim" one night if he persisted in his habits, but it was Lynn who took the swim. Heading down the dock on her way to the store at two in the morning, Lynn miscalculated the location of the ninety-degree turn and walked off the dock into the water. Fortunately she

67

Jennis Bay, about 1987. The Grumman Goose on the right was a Weldwood Canada aircraft flown by my friend Bill Cove. I was flying Weldwood's Cessna 206, parked behind the Goose. The camp belonged ton Irv Olsen, a logging contractor. It was here, years earlier, that I has first met Jerry Major.

68

was able to grab the dock and pull herself back up—no small feat, because the floats are quite high out of the water and it was pitch-black on that night. Lynn was truly lucky. She informed me about her adventure the next morning, and we agreed that even had she yelled I would not have heard her. We also agreed then not to walk the planks alone at night.

A bizarre event took place at Sullivan while I was living there, presumably protecting Ed's daughter from harm: she had an incident with an axe murderer. It was very clear and considerably warmer on this Sunday morning, when a large sea-going tug docked at Sullivan. I was on the fuel dock, messing around with the plane, and took little notice of the ship or of the two men who got off and walked down to the lodge. I noticed them talking to Lynn in front of the building. Then one man returned to the tug, which immediately went into reverse and backed off the dock. The wash from the big boat rocked the plane first, and soon the chain of docks started to buck and jackknife as the vessel picked up speed and, without the customary seaman's courtesy, plowed out of the bay with a bone in its teeth. "Somebody's in a hurry," I thought, resuming my task of cleaning the plane.

A few minutes later, a fourteen-foot tin boat powered with an outboard motor rattled the silence of the bay, the single occupant shutting it off and gliding to a stop on our dock in front of the lodge. This boater also got out and entered the building. That would be a logger from McKenzie Sound, I thought, probably wanting Lynn to open the store for him. I continued with my work until I had the aircraft shipshape for my next passengers, when I noticed Lynn and the man from the tin skiff walking up the dock toward me.

"Jack," said Lynn, "you're not going to believe this. We have a convicted axe murderer here at Sullivan Bay." I was, of course, incredulous as she continued: "That tug that was here dropped off one of the crew who was giving them some trouble. He's supposed to stay here until they come back for him in a couple of days. It just so happens that this man recognized him." Lynn gestured toward the logger who stood with us beside the plane.

"It's true," he said. "As soon as I walked into the lodge I recognized him. He comes from Lund, which is where I live. He was accused of murdering his wife with an axe. It was in all the papers. They know he did it, but he got off on some technicality. He's a crazy man. You don't want him around here." Lynn then explained to me that she had tried to call the Mounties, but having

70

the radio phone right there in the lodge where the axe murderer was sitting made it a little risky, so she aborted that plan. Lynn then proposed that I fly the guy over to Port Hardy, or even back to Lund. "Just get him out of here."

No way did I want to spend an hour and a half in an airplane with a deranged person. The memory of carrying a knife-wielding, drunken logger was still fresh in my memory. "I've got a better idea," I responded. "I'll leave you two here to keep him happy, and I'll go and get the cops." Chicken-hearted as that may seem, it proved to be the best idea, and the logger, who was pretty tough, agreed to ride shotgun until I got back.

"Two policemen will be waiting for you on the dock," said the voice in my earphones as I tracked past Numass Island, inbound for the Hardy Bay seaplane dock. The tower operator, Roy Koch, at Port Hardy airport had listened to my bizarre story about the madman at Sullivan Bay with great patience, never betraying the slightest disbelief. He had called the Mounties for us and now added to his message that "they will be in plain clothes," a fact to which I could now attest—there at the end of the seaplane dock, as I taxied in, were two big cops in mufti.

"We know who he is," was the response from the front-seat policeman.

"The reason that tug put him ashore was because he went berserk and took a fire axe to the wheel house. They weren't doing you any favours, leaving him there. We'll look after him," he assured me.

When we landed at Sullivan Bay, the two policemen walked down the dock to the lodge. If they had been wearing their red serge outfits complete with Stetsons, they couldn't have looked more like cops. They took our man into custody and plunked him in the back seat of the plane, and we flew back to Port Hardy. If this was an axe murderer, he had been a pussycat at Sullivan. I was almost convinced that he was harmless until I heard, the next morning, that he had broken out of the Port Hardy jail and was again at large. We prayed that he hadn't taken a fancy to Sullivan Bay.

71

7

BMO – Deaf and Dumb

"Get somebody with big balls to fly that airplane to Vancouver!" Vern Kemp instructed me over the phone. He was referring to the waterlogged BMO, which had been stripped of its battery, upholstery and all flight and engine instruments following an unfortunate dunking in Hardy Bay by a part-time pilot I had recently fired. "Get somebody with *great big* balls," he laughed.

I first met Pat Finnerty when I purchased my Cessna 172, OQU. Pat had been flying it for a Campbell River company, and it was he who turned over the logbooks and introduced me to the airplane. Since then we had met, off and on, at the seaplane base at the Campbell River spit and had become friends. I got to know him even better during those terrible days at Sullivan Bay following Mike Whitehead's fatal crash, which left his widow, Lynn, with the job of running the resort by herself.

Pat Finnerty had been a constant source of help for the beleaguered young widow. He helped her through some trying events relating to the salvage of Mike's plane, the coroner's jury, impending lawsuits and a series of mechanical and electrical problems that kept cropping up at the camp. Meanwhile, he was making a living flying his Cessna 180 for several companies, including a tire manufacturer and a fishing company. If he wasn't out selling truck tires in the logging camps, he would be off spotting herring for the fishing outfit, and on the way up or down the coast he would drop in at Sullivan Bay to lend a hand. He was a hell of a good pilot, and he fit Vern Kemp's description to a T.

"Did the engineer who worked on BMO after the sinking know how to purge the fuel system in a Cessna?" Pat's first question indicated that he doubted that it had been done right. "You have to take the bladders right out of the wing." He went on to explain: "Those bladders in a Cessna are dome-fastened inside the wing at the factory. The first time you put gas in them, the sloshing around of the fuel unbuttons a lot of those things, and the rubber fuel tank develops ripples along the bottom. If there's water in the fuel tank, it hides behind those ripples. You can drain the tank till hell freezes over, but you won't get that water out. I don't trust any dry-land engineer to know that." This was Pat's way of saying yes to my request that he deliver BMO to Vancouver in its present state, without instruments or radios, it having been fished out of Hardy Bay and made ready for the ferry flight by the airline's engineer.

Pat was available to do the job right away, so we filled four jerry cans with 130-octane avgas, and borrowing a boat battery from Lynn at Sullivan Bay to jury-rig into the sick airplane, we flew XRK over to Hardy Bay, where BMO waited on the dock. Our plan was to fly both airplanes back to Sullivan Bay from Hardy Bay, a short ten-minute flight, then refuel and head for Vancouver early the next morning. We would fly down the coast in formation, at a safe altitude and over waterways that would allow for a forced landing if problems arose. I would be flying shotgun in XRK to rescue Pat should anything go awry.

Since Pat would not have any communication with me or the ground stations, an arrangement with Vancouver

air traffic control was required to allow BMO into the Vancouver traffic pattern. Known as "nordo" (no radio), this sort of flight is not uncommon, and provisions are made by Transport Canada officials through the use of a "ferry permit" authorized by the air transport authorities with the engineer who has signed out the aircraft as being airworthy. It would be our responsibility to arrange with the Vancouver tower the approval for all radio communication to be handled by me in XRK, and Pat would simply follow me and manoeuvre in a like fashion.

On our arrival at Hardy Bay, we jury-rigged the battery in place and dumped the twenty gallons of fuel into BMO—ten gallons per wing tank. While the airplane would start satisfactorily, Pat was still skeptical about how the engineer had purged the water from the fuel system. I had the little sample cup in hand and stabbed it into the fuel-bleed valve of the left wing tank and came up with 100 percent water. I did it again, and then again, and still no sign of the green 130 octane fuel.

"Holy smoke, Pat, this thing is full of water," I exclaimed, taking another contaminated sample from the tank. We located a quart jar from a fisherman and took a full quart of water out of the tank before a telltale sample of gasoline showed up. After that, each test revealed total fuel without any unwelcome water in the fuel, even after rocking the wings of the aircraft at the dock. We then checked the belly drain for the left fuel tank and determined that no water remained in the lines, so the left tank was clear.

"I don't care about the right tank for now," Pat insisted. "Let's get the left side completely clear before worrying about the right one." He decided to take the aircraft up for a test flight and during the flight to waggle his wings in order to shake any water hiding behind those little ripples that he insisted were in the bottom of each rubber tank. During an earlier conversation with the engineer I had been told, unequivocally, that the fuel system had been purged: "There is no water in those tanks."

Now, nearly two quarts of water later, we were about to make a test flight—so much for "unequivocal" engineers. The Cessna taxied away from the dock into fairly rough water created by a gusty wind blowing into Hardy Bay. The heavy chop created a lot of wing-waggling, and while taxiing, BMO backfired and coughed and wouldn't take power when Pat tried to open the throttle. He returned BMO, belching and backfiring, to the dock, where we drained out yet another pint of water from the left tank— Finnerty's "ripples" were now a reality.

Three test flights were made that afternoon, drawing fuel from the left tank. Two deadstick landings resulted from power failure due to more water appearing in that left bladder. The right tank didn't yield as much trouble, and we were soon ready to fly back to Sullivan Bay, where we would fill all the tanks in preparation for the morning's flight. The morning dawned clear but very gusty, with a thirty-knot headwind in the forecast for the flight down Johnstone Strait. We taxied out in unison from the dock at Sullivan Bay and took off together into the gusty southeaster. Both aircraft carried full tanks, but the reduced weight of BMO—with all but the pilots seat removed and no instruments or gear—gave her an advantage, and she pulled ahead of me in the climbout. We were in formation by the time we reached Simoom Sound and proceeded down Johnstone Strait, past Campbell River and on past Texada Island into the Strait of Georgia, right on the money with respect to our ETA as flight-planned.

Prior to takeoff, we had telephoned our flight plan and had made the necessary arrangements with the Vancouver tower to facilitate the acceptance of a "nordo" aircraft into Vancouver airspace. At Gower Point, I called the tower and identified XRK as being in company with BMO, who was deaf and dumb—he would do whatever I did. The tower operator had been waiting for us and knew all about it, and we were cleared direct to the Iona Jetty via Point Grey. The Iona Jetty is a long rockpile extending from Iona Island, in the mouth of the north arm of the Fraser River, out to sea for about three miles. The heavily silted river mouth creates a shoal for this entire distance, and the rip-rap of the jetty is above water for the entire distance. The wall forms a very visible reporting point for aircraft inbound from the northwest and is parallel to the approach for the main west-east runway used by the heavies at Vancouver's busy airport when the southeast wind prevails.

All went well until we got to the Iona Jetty, when all hell broke loose. It seems the tower operator handling us from Gower Point to the jetty did not pass on the full information when handing us off to the airport traffic controller, who didn't know that we were two aircraft acting as one. This operator called me and stated, "Please hold north of the jetty—heavy on final." A Boeing 747 was three miles back for runway 08, and the tower was telling me to stay put until further notice. I looked over to my right and back, and there was BMO holding station very nicely. When I commenced my holding turn to the left, I saw Pat's

wing come up obediently, to follow, so I knew he understood. I then directed my attention to my own business, leaving Pat to his. But when I had completed the turn and looked back again, he was gone. Expecting to see the familiar orange snout of the 185, I hauled my aircraft around through a 360-degree turn, but the sky was empty.

"XRK, what is your position?" The tower operator's voice came through my headphones with a strong indication of concern. He asked me to squawk ident, which required that I push a little button on my transponder, which in turn caused the tower's radar blip of XRK to "bloom," showing my exact position. I was still north of the jetty as required, so the next transmission came in a puzzled tone: "Did you see another airplane, very low on the shoreline?" I indicated that I had lost sight of my travelling companion, who had no communication, and perhaps it had been him.

The revelation that he had a "nordo" aircraft operating in the circuit must have come as a nasty surprise to the tower operator, but since there was no other reason to hold me in position, he cleared me across the button of 08 to land on the river. As I flared XRK onto the river at the Vancouver seaplane base, I was relieved to see the distinctive colours of BMO sitting proud at the top of the seaplane ramp. There was a figure leaning against the port-side float: the redoubtable Pat Finnerty had somehow made it.

I docked my airplane at the public seaplane wharf and ran up the ramp over to BMO. Pat didn't move from his leaning position against the pontoon—he was white in the face and taking deep drags from a cigarette. He didn't wait for the question, he just gave me the answer. "Back at Gower Point, I switched tanks. The headwind down the coast cost me a lot of fuel, and the left tank was dry when I switched over to the full right tank. Everything was fine until I followed you into that left turn near the jetty," he recalled, still working on the remains of his smoke while slowly gaining composure.

"When that right wing went up, the engine gulped some more of that bloody water and she quit. I pointed the plane back toward the ocean while spinning the fuel selector back to left tank, pumping the throttle full and trying to get that engine started. I was heading right for the rocks of the jetty and couldn't do anything about it. She came down on that crazy water like a ton of bricks and bounced twenty feet into the air. The next landing was going to be onto those damned rocks, but just at that moment she caught, backfiring and belching, but with enough power to get over that rock pile

before she quit again and I hammered into those waves on the other side."

At this point, Pat made some reference to becoming religious, then continued: "When I hit the second time, I knew she wouldn't take those seas—that shallow water was wild. I spun the fuel selector, blindly, back and forth, and pumped the throttle. She fired and held power." Pat took the last drag from his smoke and recounted how, once having regained power, he pointed the airplane at the seaplane base and, with an understandable panic now fully developed, simply arrowed the airplane to the safety of the river. "I went right over the button of 08, and there was no 747 in my way at ten feet off the deck," he laughed, referring to my explanation for the turn.

"I didn't even throttle back for the landing, and I just drove this sucker straight up the seaplane ramp," he admitted. "When I reached the top of the ramp she quit again, and I didn't give a damn. But when I looked down at that fuel selector, you won't believe where it was positioned—it was selected in the 'both off' position. Figure that one!" I never did figure out why that engine had kept running for three minutes with the fuel shut off, but I did come to another conclusion: Pat Finnerty sure fit Vern Kemp's job description.

8

XRK – One Black One Green

Dr. Vern Kemp, my friend and partner from Port Hardy, had been advised by his accountant that his airline capers were costing him big bucks. The doctor didn't need an accountant to tell him this. I think his wife, his barber or even the family dog could have advised him, if his love of flying had made him miss the obvious. So, I was not surprised to receive another one of those "call me on a land line" messages.

Considering that the man had not yet seen a fair return on his investment and had suffered the sinking of his favourite airplane, it was no great shock to me that Vern had decided to go back to something straightforward like brain surgery. He made me a generous offer, that I take over the ownership of XRK at a very fair price and continue, alone, with the application for the charter licence. The operative word in this agreement was "alone," and we parted amicably with the plan that his accountant would draw up an agreement of

sale for XRK. We would then get together to complete the transaction.

In the meantime, I was putting both airplanes to good use. A pilot friend, Peter, had come to fly with me and had brought with him a contract with a fish-packing company near Campbell River. We were to rendezvous early each morning with two prawn boats and fly their catch to the packing house. One boat was fishing in Clio Channel near Minstrel Island, and the other was located near Sullivan Bay. Peter, who lived in Campbell River, was keeping one of the planes there and servicing the closer prawn boat at Minstrel Island each morning while I stayed at Sullivan Bay picking up from the northern boat.

By ten o'clock each morning we would complete the prawn haul and then meet at Sullivan Bay to clean up the airplanes, put the seats back in and resume charter flights for the day. Although they were packed in large,

I loved this airplane: XRK taxiing out of Shawl Bay.

called for an eight o'clock delivery, which had to be moved up to nine-thirty in order to give the pilot some daylight for his takeoff. More often than not, Peter's flight up to Minstrel Island and back was performed a few feet off the water in conditions of minimum acceptable visibility. He was doing all the prawn hauls at this point because the Minstrel Island boat was the only one working, and it too would soon be shutting down for the winter.

Although the revenue generated from the prawn hauls was welcome, we were not unhappy that the job would soon be over for the season. I was looking forward to consummating the purchase of XRK and getting on with the pursuit of a scheduled licence out of Campbell River and a base at Sullivan Bay. Vern's earlier work had put this application in motion with the Canadian Transport Commission, and some follow-up was now needed. Working, as we were, for another operator had distinct disadvantages for both parties, but with any luck we could be in business on our own hook by the next season.

"With any luck" was not quite how things turned out. The day had dawned blustery with rain showers at my home in Qualicum Beach, where I had spent the weekend. BMO had been left at the dock in Deep Bay, where it had

sealed plastic containers, the prawns tended to be a bit stinky, so we gave considerable attention to keeping the airplanes clean for our passengers. When the prawn hauls started to taper off and only the Minstrel Island boat was producing a load, XRK was chosen to do the fish run so that when BMO was returned to Vern, it would be daisy fresh.

The weather on the coast can get pretty ugly in mid-January, and those early morning flights to the prawn boat were becoming a problem. The contract remained over the two-day holiday. On this morning my son, planning to spend some time with me at Sullivan Bay, had joined me in the plane for the eight-thirty takeoff. We had not gone far up the island shoreline before he commented that it wasn't much of a day. I had to agree, because we were getting kicked around pretty badly. As we flew past the Campbell River spit we noticed that all the airlines' docks were full of airplanes, which was a good indicator that the weather was pretty awful up the coast.

Pressing on up Johnstone Strait, we didn't get past the cable crossing at Discovery Narrows before it became evident that this was no day for flying airplanes. Heavy snow and driving winds turned us back and we landed in the river at the spit, taxiing up to the Freshwater Marina, where Peter usually docked XRK. I was surprised and a little concerned that the familiar 185 was not in its place on the dock and asked the dock attendant if he knew anything about it. "Peter took off about seven this morning," he said. "He was going somewhere to drop a passenger. I didn't get all the details."

I picked up the phone from the desk and called Peter's home, getting his wife, Donna, out of her sickbed. "I'm not working today, I've got a lousy cold," she said. "Peter left early. He had

a passenger lined up for a trip up near Warner Bay; then he was to going pick up the prawns and head down." Donna showed concern when I told her we had not been able to make it up Johnstone Strait, but I assured her that the weather must have been better at the time of Peter's departure and that he was probably sitting somewhere, holding for weather. It was our established procedure to leave a company flight note on these occasions, and Donna read it to me.

The flight note stated that Peter would be dropping a passenger at a tugboat in Warner Bay before picking up the prawns. Since it was now nine-thirty, I calculated that he would have had time to make Warner Bay and get back to the boat at Minstrel. Telephoning the fish packer, I received the message that "the prawn boat just called us, wondering when to expect the plane." Now I was concerned.

I called Sullivan Bay, which is on the way to Warner Bay, but couldn't raise the camp watcher. Then I contacted the logging operation at Boughey Bay as well as Hadley Bay. Both were located in Savannah Channel, where Peter would have flown on his way up the coast. Neither of them had heard a plane.

"It started snowing here a while ago. Nobody is flying in this," reported the

82

timekeeper at Boughey Bay. I told him I was concerned that Peter might have landed and be taxiing the channel in search of a safe berth or be heeled up on a beach close by. By this time the operators of the Freshwater Marina, all friends of Peter's and concerned for him, had given me the use of the owner's house, which had two telephone lines: one would be used for outgoing calls and one held for incoming calls.

I was now getting scared. Although I didn't want to frighten Donna I knew that if Peter were to call, he would contact her first, and I wanted to be sure she knew where to reach me. When I talked to her, she made it clear that she was in the picture. She seemed to be in control but I was concerned for her, sitting alone there in the couple's apartment, sweating out this worst possible situation.

The prawn boat at Minstrel Island had been asked to patrol Savannah Channel in case Peter was caught in the heavy snowstorm that had now developed. The search-and-rescue people at Comox had long been alerted and had called back for more information when, suddenly, the phone reserved for incoming calls rang.

Pat Finnerty was on the line. He had run into someone from the marina and had been told of the crisis—could he help? I asked him if he would go to

Peter's apartment and keep Donna company until we received some news, at which time I would meet him there. Another call came in from the search-and-rescue squadron indicating that they had located an airplane taxiing in bad weather near Powell River—could that be our aircraft?

"Not likely," we advised. Later, they called back to confirm that it had been another airplane. It was now past noon, and the situation was grave. I asked my son to man the two phones and redirect calls to Donna's home, where I joined her and Pat to wait. We sat around, drinking coffee and making reassuring conversation. Donna was still outwardly very confident and stated that she and Peter had talked about the possibility of this happening. She knew he would take every precaution and would get in touch as soon as possible. We all agreed that Peter knew the coast too well to get suckered in by this weather.

Time crawled by, the passage of each hour reducing the likelihood of the whole thing being a mistake. Then a phone call came in, at about two-thirty: "We have located a downed aircraft, and a Canadian Forces Buffalo aircraft is on its way to the scene. That's all I can tell you, sir. Yes, it's in the general vicinity of Minstrel Island. We will call as soon as we know." This call drained the emotion from everyone in the

A sad ending for
XRK. PAT FINNERTY
PHOTO

room. Here was confirmation that Peter was down—it wasn't, after all, just a slip-up, a misunderstanding. He wasn't sitting somewhere drinking coffee, holding for weather. Our conversation stopped.

An hour later, search-and-rescue phoned again: "Two para-rescue medics have jumped into the crash site, sir— they report one black one green. That means one person has been found dead and the other alive. Sorry, sir, we don't know which—passenger or pilot. We will call you the minute we know."

Donna served us all coffee, and we slumped into our seats in stunned silence. I was seated in the armchair beside the telephone—I didn't want it to ring again. Less than an hour later,

it ignored my wishes and rang. The instrument was heavier than it had been on previous calls, but I lifted it and listened.

"Good news for you, sir—your pilot's alive!" The three of us hugged.

The news came out in bits and pieces from different sources: the crash site was revealed as Burial Cove, just a quarter mile in a straight line from Minstrel Island and the last turn in Savannah Channel before reaching Minstrel Island. An aircraft leaving Port Hardy airport at one o'clock had been the true saviour. Listening on the distress frequency, the pilot had picked up XRK's electronic locator transmitter signal, which had turned on with the crash impact. The pilot, totally in cloud with no visibility of the ground, had homed in on the transmission, estab- lished the coordinates and radioed them back to Port Hardy tower. He was the first of three men whose actions saved Peter's life.

A search-and-rescue Buffalo aircraft on its way back to Comox from the Yukon was redirected to the site. Two para-rescue medics jumped blind through the heavy overcast and landed directly at the crash scene. One of the jumpers, the jump master himself, broke both of his ankles from his descent through trees, leaving a junior man, who was experiencing his first "hot"

doctor stated that the para-rescue medic's handling of the injured man had saved his life.

The duty doctor on that day was a physician from Port Hardy who, when stepping from the helicopter at the crash site, was overwhelmed to find that the totally destroyed aircraft was his own and that the badly injured pilot, now wrapped in bandages, splints and blankets and secured for transport, was virtually unidentifiable, but it was either me or Peter, who flew for the airline to whom he leased the aircraft. Only later, on the helicopter returning to the hospital, did Dr. Vern Kemp, our erstwhile partner, determine that Peter was his critically injured patient.

The fatally injured passenger, a tugboat owner, had been returning to one of his ships in Warner Bay. He had been interested in purchasing a house in Burial Cove and had asked Peter to take a turn over it as they flew up the channel. It was during this inspection, which took place in blustery but relatively clear weather conditions, that the crash occurred, instantly killing the passenger.

When the wreck was inspected, Peter's David Clarke headset was found imbedded in the instrument panel. The radio knobs had penetrated an inch and a quarter into the headset case upon the initial impact. David Clarke proved to be the first person to save Peter's life.

XRK's cockpit was drenched with fuel from the crumpled wing, but there was no fire.

jump to a real accident site, to attend to Peter as well as his own colleague.

Peter had been lying in the wreckage, on top of one of the floats, for over eight hours. He had multiple injuries, as well as hypothermia from the hellish weather. When the helicopter arrived with the provincial rescue team's duty doctor aboard, the

9

ON THE LAM

"George has to have the best of every-thing," said Phil Melly, the company's master mechanic, as he loaded two massive tool kits into the back of the Cessna. He was referring to the air-plane—it was a beauty.

I had been highly recommended for this job, and they had been highly recommended to me. Schneider, the road-building former pilot, had been the object of high recommendations. Phil, my first manager in the new job, set me straight.

"Don't let it go to your head," he laughed. "Robert wanted out, fast, so that he could take a good job with Air BC." The mechanic betrayed a slight Irish brogue in his speech and an engaging twinkle in his eye. Over the next year, he would prove to be my mentor and confidant, because I would be flying him from one job site to the next for my new employer, George,

owner of LTJ Contracting, a builder of logging roads.

"That's the name this week, anyway," Phil twinkled as Bill Foyle slid the float dolly between the 2960s and signalled for us to get aboard. We were about to be dollied to the seaplane ramp at Vancouver airport for my inaugural flight as the "corporate pilot" of this company. We were heading up to the Campbell River office, from which the firm operated eleven road projects with a variety of logging companies around the coast. As we were dropped onto the planks of the ramp, Bill, the engineer from Aeroflight who had just performed the hundred-hour check on ERQ, called out, "Don't bend any cabin braces, Jack!" He then sped off in the float dolly, leaving me a little baffled about that remark. Turning to Phil to ask what it was all about, I found the little Irishman bobbing his head up and down and chuckling. "You'll find out

87

Facing page: A row of Beavers on the Nanaimo seaplane dock. The front one is being warmed up for a flight to Vancouver harbour.
BRIAN SCHOFIELD PHOTO

soon enough," he laughed, as we motored down the ramp into the Fraser River.

The colour scheme on CF-ERQ, the company's Cessna 185, was quite elegant. I remarked on this to Phil an hour later, as we taxied upriver to the Freshwater Marina at Campbell River. "Champagne-and-tan, George calls it," said Phil, as we loaded his tool kits into the back of a Honda that had been waiting for us at the top of the ramp. The little truck had the same colour scheme as the plane. "This will be your vehicle," explained Phil, who had described to me the nature of my job during our flight up from town. "You'll be running parts and tools and powder and groceries back and forth from the dock to the various camps. And people, of course. Me and Arnold and the powder man mostly, and the various machine operators. On a good day, George and Terry and Shirley"—more head bobbing and chuckles. I had the feeling there were a few unstated things in store for me.

When we got to the company office and equipment yard, Phil ushered me into the front office, where I was introduced to George. "George, this is your new pilot. His name's Jack, and he seems to know his way from town." Phil ducked out, leaving me to shake hands with a very large man seated at a mag-

nificent rosewood desk. George's hand felt like a ham as he held me in his somewhat clammy grip. He was not fat, but he was mighty big, and I immediately sized him up as full gross in a Cessna 185.

Before speaking, George suddenly cleared his nose and the back of his throat with a loud horking sound. This startled me; I thought he was going gather it all up and spit, but he didn't. I was to learn that this was a nervous habit George indulged in about every eight minutes. I looked around to see if that funny little Irishman was looking in on us as George spoke: "So, you've got lots of flying experience around these parts, eh?"

I explained that I had been flying with a small airline up the coast, but George cut me off, more interested in what he had to say than in listening to me. "Robert was the best pilot I ever had, except for maybe John. Do you know John Hann?"

"Yes, I do know John. He and I . . ."

"We used to fly the ass off John with the other company. We had twenty-three jobs underway, turned two mil a year at that time. Not so much now, but it'll get better. That guy down at Aeroflight? What's his name?"

"Uh, Bill? Bill Foyle?"

"Yeah, Foyle. He opened the door of ERQ early one morning, and John fell

out—Ha! He'd been so burnt out he just slept all night in the plane. Did you know John?"

"Yes, I . . ."

"Have you met Arnold?" George was gesturing at the guy seated over in the corner at a small, beaten-up desk. Arnold got up and we shook hands. George horked.

"Arnold goes under the title of time-keeper, but he does everything around here. That right, Arnold?"

Arnold didn't look up. "That's right, George."

George horked, then bellowed— "Shirley! Come and meet your new pilot." Shirley came in with the son, Terry. As a group, we now had a Beaver load.

The family stood around for a few minutes, just smiling at me and making small talk, the gist of which was that the important part of my job was to fly them all down to Pitt Meadows every Friday night and to bring them all back on Monday morning.

"You don't have to worry about us," said Terry—"us" being he and Cindy, a pretty little thing who now waved at me from her desk in the other room— "we're living here in Campbell."

"Yeah," laughed George. "They're just married and living on the fruits of love. Isn't that right, Cindy?" Cindy waved, smiling, and George horked. "Well, stop

Facing page: ERQ coming up the ramp at the Freshwater Marina in Campbell River. Terry Hutchinson and my daughter, Liz, with me watching.

leaving the banana peels around, then," he called out, guffawing and expecting everyone to join him. At that moment Phil the mechanic walked through the corridor and flashed me one of his Irish grins.

It was decided to send me into Jackson Bay, where they were building a road. Arnold needed the time cards picked up, there was a case of oil for one of the machines and when I was through there I was to scoot up Lough-borough Inlet to Tower Point, across from Apple River, and bring out a troublesome catskinner.

I was flying a clean, well-maintained airplane in my old stamping grounds and getting paid for it, so what was there to complain about?

During the first week of flying for LTJ Contracting, the weather was superb and I was kept busy servicing the camps in Wakeman Sound, Tower Point and Jackson Bay. Occasionally I picked up breakdown parts from the local branch of Finning Tractor or a case or two of "Forcite" from the powder magazine atop the hill behind Campbell River. I paid cash for many of these purchases, right from George's ample wallet, and more by osmosis than as a result of direct statements from anyone, I determined that George wasn't exactly the best credit risk in town. The eleven jobs underway were

what was left of the twenty-six contracts my new employer referred to quite regularly as the "good old days."

I concluded that the good old days ended up as the bad old days when George lost control of one side of the general ledger—the spending side. He bought vehicles like he had stock in General Motors, and Phil confided that at one time George had six brand-new private vehicles for his own and his son's use. The company equipment, from air compressors to the big Hitachi power shovels, looked like they had just come off a parade square. They were immaculately maintained and kept bright and clean and were replaced earlier in their life than was usual in this business. "You'll not have to worry about getting any work done on the airplane, Jack," said Phil. "Particularly since George has to fly in it."

I flew George for the first time that week. He was terrified of flying and told me right off that he became a "basket case" when in the air. This surprised me, because the log entries from the previous pilots indicated that he flew with them quite often. "It's the only way for me to get around, but I hate it," replied George, who had climbed into the right seat and had taken a firm grip on the cabin brace. Suddenly, as we taxied down the river, he pulled his hand off the brace as if he

ON THE LAM

had been burned. "Oops," he exclaimed, "I'm not supposed to hang on to this—it costs me three hundred bucks every time I break it."

So *that* was it. I recalled Bill Foyle's parting words in Vancouver. George revealed to me that he had pulled the cabin brace right out of the plane and bent it beyond repair on two occasions. The man must have weighed in at three hundred pounds plus, and he had developed the habit of hanging on to the brace with both hands during take-off. The four little screws positioning the V-shaped windshield brace just couldn't take George's weight.

It was a beautiful day, with the water beneath us sparkling in the sunshine. The scene unfolding beneath the belly of ERQ was unquestionably the most beautiful in the world. I looked over to George to share my thoughts when I realized he was not taking in the scenery. He was sitting bolt upright in controlled terror. When the aircraft banked left, George banked right; when we descended, George leaned back; and in a climb he was to be witnessed straining forward against his seat belt, all in a vain attempt to keep the world as George wanted it rather than as it was. He had trained himself not to go with the airplane.

I had flown many people who fought the airplane like George. These were the passengers who invariably pitched their biscuit when the weather got rough; they were so busy trying to keep themselves at right angles to the plane that their guts just gave up. A former neighbour who was captain of the *Empress of Canada* said the same of passengers at sea. "The ones that get sea-sick plan it that way," he once told me.

We landed at Jackson Bay, and George had me drive the company pickup truck on the logging road up to Seabird Lake, where one of the company's Hitachi shovels was having problems. The road was long and winding and frequented by loaded logging trucks hurtling down to the log dump. We monitored a constant patter of position reports from the trucks as we made our way up the road, and we transmitted our position to them as well, referring, as we drove, to the road mileage indicators installed for that purpose. When a truck got close to us, we would dart into one of the many pull-offs and wait for it to go thundering by, usually blowing its air horn as it passed and leaving us covered in white dust.

The Hitachi's problem was that the right-of-way for the new section of road had proven to be solid granite, and some drilling and blasting would be required before its services would be needed. The operator of the shovel was angry at George and confided to me,

92

"He's the typical low bidder—just get the job at any price, then worry about details later." The shovel operator knew that he would now be laid off while this section was properly prepared for his work. Meanwhile, George talked, with great animation, to the logging contractor, trying to get a cost concession out of him.

"When we did our estimates," he explained, "there was snow on this section. You know how that can be deceiving. We just need about a buck forty-two a yard more for just this short section—it doesn't extend more than six hundred feet. Then, it will be back to normal." Phil Melly, my Irish friend, used to describe George on these occasions as "George talking in earnest," because it happened often enough to be considered amusing.

In the plane on the way back, George was philosophical. "It works, sometimes," he laughed. "What you lose on the short haul you pick up in the long run." George horked, then reached for the cabin brace, stopping himself with a resigned laugh as we took off.

The next week I flew several planeloads of powder to the Jackson Bay job. This task entailed driving the truck up to the powder magazine and transferring only the exact number of cases that it was possible to carry in the plane. Regulations about leaving this stuff around were understandably strict, and passengers in the plane were required to be only company employees with a good reason to be aboard. Blasting caps, which are more dangerous than the powder, were not to be carried at the same time as the dynamite—a rule I didn't find hard to follow, because caps have been known to go off from stray radio transmissions.

The company blaster, however, seemed slightly deranged. "All blasters are crazy," Arnold advised. "Take him up on the next powder trip and leave him at the job. He's got work to do."

The blaster was the most high-strung guy I'd ever met, in a laid-back kind of way—if that makes sense. Around powder he was totally indifferent. "It just burns," he said, as we flew along.

"Everybody figures it's going to blow up—it just burns—it takes a cap or a detonation to make it go bang. It just burns. You could slam into that mountain and we would just burn, except," he said, with a sly grin, "these here would make us go bang." He reached under his seat and revealed a box of caps, which he had secretly slipped aboard with the powder. "Ya better not hit that mountain after all—ha, ha!"

I transported about ten planeloads of powder that week, flying with the windows open to get rid of the smell of the nitro. I found that breathing the fumes

FLIGHTS OF A COAST DOG

"Champagne and tan" was the colour of all the roadbuilding equipment at LTJ Contracting, including the company Cessna 185. ERQ was first owned by Hyack Air, then sold to Maple Ridge Construction, which became LTJ Construction and then Rainbow Mountain Road Builders, which sold ERQ before going out of business. Later, when owned by Ash River Investments, it turned turtle in French Creek. A passenger who had also escaped from a fatal twin Otter crash in Vancouver harbour was aboard and had to swim to shore. He complained that he had made two water takeoffs but never a landing.

caused an instant "high," with an attendant red flush to the face and chest palpitations—not good symptoms for a pilot. A doctor friend advised me that nitroglycerine was used for heart stimulation, so I was looking forward to the last load. Before that happened, however, one more adventure was to occur.

ERQ was due for its one-hundred-hour check, and, true to form, George had wrenched the cabin brace out of kilter. The plane had to go in for this servicing, but demand for the powder at Jackson Bay had a high priority. There was also a lot of work for the airplane at the other camps. George came to the rescue by borrowing a Cessna 206 from a friend who flew for one of the major airlines. I flew ERQ to Vancouver for service and picked up the 206 at Pitt Meadows.

Private airplanes do not get the attention received by working aircraft, and this 206, although seemingly okay, had not been maintained anything like ERQ. Unbeknown to anyone, the fuel-injection system was in distress. With the first load of powder aboard, and the blaster as well, we landed at Jackson Bay and taxied to the dock. I pulled the mixture control, switched off and jumped out to tie up the plane. My blaster friend, still seated in the co-pilot seat, called out to me, "Hey, we're on fire!" He slid out as I tied off the rope

and jumped back aboard, grabbing the fire extinguisher from under the pilot seat. He pointed toward the engine on the right side, so I slid across and stepped out on the outboard float.

Sure enough, there was a fire inside the engine cowling, and the paint on the cowling was ablaze—a small fire, but spreading rapidly up the cowling. It was comforting to have been previously assured that the dynamite aboard would only burn. I let go with the fire extinguisher inside the cowling and then against the burning paint. The fire went out very quickly and had not, apparently, done any damage, except to the paint job. I removed the cowling and inspected what is loosely referred to as the "octopus," which is the distribution system for this fuel-injected engine. There was a slight fuel leak at the primer pump connection that I was able to tighten after removing the locking wire, but other than that, I had no idea what had ignited the gas.

With some apprehension, I flew the 206 back to Campbell River, where a mechanic took a look at it. He couldn't come up with any more evidence than I had, so I flew the plane back to Vancouver and traded it for ERQ, which was now ready. Later, the owner of the 206 phoned me and chewed me out for treating his airplane so badly. A few days later he phoned back and

95

apologized: the problem had been diagnosed, and he was told that he was lucky the whole thing hadn't gone up in smoke. *He* was lucky?

I was well treated by George and his family during those days, and the employees were all good people to work with. Flying George and Shirley back to Pitt Meadows on Fridays could be something of a trial, because they preferred that I stay with them all weekend at their home rather than go back and forth, burning the hours on the company aircraft. My family were in Qualicum Beach, so the idea of spending my weekends as a house guest at Pitt Meadows wasn't a big hit. It happened only on one occasion, during which I was regaled with the account of how George beat cancer. Although it was a true account of how he had been classified as terminal and somehow beat the rap (laetrile in Mexico, he swore, did the trick), it was nevertheless a boring way to spend two days. I thought this might explain why the previous pilot had slept in the plane. With winter approaching, George and Shirley solved the problem by taking an apartment in Campbell River.

The number of camps we were operating slipped from eleven to six, then down to three. There was a certain tension in the air as the equipment from the completed jobs came home to Campbell River and then, somehow, just disappeared. One of the big Hitachis was seized by the distributor, and four of the pickups were driven off somewhere. Nobody was building roads at this time of year, and George could be described as having a hunted look as his business started to fall apart.

One morning, I came in to the office and was greeted with the news that I no longer worked for LTJ Contracting. George roared with laughter: "Did you see his face? You're working for Rainbow Mountain Road Builders, now," he laughed. "You figured we'd fired you, didn't you?" He then went on to explain that all the new work would be taken on under the name of the new company. He also warned me to stay away from well-populated places while flying the airplane. "How is that Deep Bay near your house for an airplane?" he asked. I explained that it was a very small harbour, with a few fishing boats and some private homes. He liked the sound of it and suggested that we keep the plane there as much as possible. I got the distinct feeling that somebody was looking for the airplane. Also, the advent of a new name, "Rainbow Mountain Road Builders," suggested that the old company was going down like the *Titanic*. Guess who came up with the title of a new hit song, "Somewhere the Rainbow's Over"?

96

Then George struck pay dirt. A Hitachi shovel working on the right-of-way at Jackson Bay cut too deeply into a bank, and a huge rock the size of a two-car garage slid down with tons of overburden and crunched the shovel. The operator miraculously got out unscathed, but the shovel was a goner, so the insurance company wrote off the shovel and paid out on the insurance. When the transaction was complete, George very casually asked the adjuster if he would take a thousand bucks for the wreck, and his offer was accepted. "I'll get some parts out of it," George said.

Phil Melly nearly collapsed in amazement when George sent him in to see the wreck, which had now been dug out and the big rock rolled back. What George had determined was that the shovel was almost intact. The rock had not fallen on the shovel but had merely rolled up against it, flattened the cab and shifted the engine a few inches to one side. Phil had the engine back in place and the cab cut off and replaced in less than two weeks, and the shovel was back to work. The value of that shovel would bail George out of the game, and that's just what he did— bail out.

Not long afterward, George took me aside and told me he would have to let the airplane go, and, of course, he wouldn't need a pilot any more. He had been very pleased with my work, and I was the best pilot he had ever had— even better than John or Robert—and it was too bad, but that's the way the cookie crumbles. He added that if I could find someone to buy the airplane, it might mean I would get a job flying it again. And that is precisely what happened.

Several years later I heard that George's luck had run out. The cancer, which had been in remission, returned. This time, the trips to Mexico didn't save him—George had bent his last cabin brace.

97

10
COMING ON SIDE

We came in overtop Link Lake. I throttled back slowly, then eased the pitch control in and screwed the vernier control up tight to hold the propeller in full fine pitch. The fuel was already selected on "Both," and the speed was bleeding off to ninety knots. I selected two notches of flap, and the "Johnson bar" locked in place with that inimitable "clack." Pam Kleven was seated beside me and was curious about "that clicking noise" made by the elevator trim wheel, which was now helping to bring up the nose and reduce our speed to eighty as we made a dramatic descent down the concrete spillway of the Ocean Falls dam.

My passengers, Ray and Pam Kleven and their son Greg, who now owned ERQ, were as impressed as was I on the first occasion of landing here in an inflow wind condition. The descent down that massive concrete spillway over the transmission cables gave one a true sense of flying and brought home

the reality of how insignificant this little airplane was in the scheme of things. We flared onto the whitecaps in front of the townsite and came off the step in time to achieve my intention of avoiding the necessity of a turn, downwind, to make it to the seaplane dock. Taxiing into the gusting wind, we came alongside and made fast on the inside of the float while the Kleven family disembarked.

I handled the airplane around onto the adjacent dock to leave room for the regular plane that based here as Ray explained, "We are probably going to be here all day, Jack, so why don't you come with us up to the hotel?" Earlier, I had been informed that the family logging company, Ash River Investments, had taken a contract here in Ocean Falls and that this day would be spent with the timber owners, walking over the site and making some preliminary decisions about moving in their equipment and setting up camp. "You

FIELD - '84

KEN SWARTZ PHOTO

might have to spend the day at the Martin Inn, counting the rosebuds on the wallpaper," laughed Greg. "But isn't that what pilots do?"

The coffee served in the Martin Inn cafe could not be described as battery acid—it was more like the "liquor" used in the rendering of wood chips in the paper mill, which was within my view as I sipped my second refill. My vagrant thoughts were interrupted by the sound of an aircraft coming down the spillway, as we had so recently done in the Cessna. A dirty yellow Beaver flared for a landing, then taxied to the dock, where the pilot performed the same docking ritual that we had, but left the airplane ready for a quick departure. He came up the ramp at a run to the street and across the roadway to the dispatch office, which was right next to the hotel. He could be picking up his next passengers or freight, or just coming in for a quick pee before heading out to Bella Bella or up to Klemtu or, perhaps, a long trip down to Port Hardy.

My idle observation of the charter pilot was carrying my thoughts, inevitably, to a subject that, until now, I had been avoiding—a recollection of times past and of a particular friend with whom I had learned to fly, spent hours in his home, hangar flying with groups of aspiring pilots; flew cross-country flights in tandem, in three and

sometimes four airplanes; scared the hell out of some fishermen on the Vedder River one day as three of us, in Tiger Moths in tight formation and three feet from the water, roared our way up to Chilliwack for an air show, where we would drop flour bombs on a target and attempt to burst balloons with the prop—a flood of memories, of faces and names, especially Bob d'Eassum.

The pilot came out of the dispatch office at a dead run. He retraced his path down the dock, cast off his one rope and jumped into the Beaver as it faded off the dock. A puff of blue exhaust was followed by the grumble of the big radial engine as the Beaver, with a killer whale painted on its rudder, taxied out and turned quickly into wind. The little silver water rudders suddenly appeared at the stern of the floats, and the engine roared into life. The Beaver was airborne in an instant, holding close to the water as the flaps bled off slowly, and then, climbing into the sou'-easter, it disappeared from my view.

As the sound of the motor receded I could envision the pilot's flight path in full view of the townsite, taking a full left turn as he came abeam the big concrete ramp used by the Mallard flying boats, into Cousins Inlet, where his sound would be swallowed by the

An aerial view of the Campbell River seaplane spit. The aircraft are visible on the Gulf Air and Island Air docks. The Freshwater Marina is located in the river arm to the right, about halfway up. Note the gravel bars in the river, which caused some concern when the tide was low. CITY OF CAMPBELL RIVER PHOTO

towering forest on each side of that narrow waterway. Still climbing, he would ultimately turn right into Gunboat Passage and would, as the newspapers had reported some twenty years earlier about Bob, "never be seen again."

Bob had been with Pacific Western Airlines in those days. His airplane was not a Beaver but a Cessna 180 similar to ERQ, which was now bobbing on the dock from the wake of that departing aircraft. It was the same dock Bob had taken off from, the same dispatch office—different faces, different names. The biggest air search ever mounted in B.C. to that date did not turn up so much as an oil slick. Bob's mother, Lille, ever-present when we future aviators were hangar-flying, was a columnist for the *Vancouver Sun*. She had put the heat on in the right places, and the search went on and on. But no broken trees, no washed-up artifact, no oil slick, provided a clue.

We stood in the pelting rain by the railing overlooking the CPR docks in Vancouver harbour, and friends gave eulogies—friends who were pilots, and at least two of whom would face the same fate. Two South Korean kids, the subject of a deportation order, whom Lille and Bob had spirited away from Canada Immigration, were there braving discovery to help cast the wreath for their missing benefactor.

The flowers hit the wall on the way down and landed, upside-down, drifting, out of sight, among the pilings under pier D. The ink on the card of remembrance would run and be illegible in an instant. We who were soaked in the downpour sought a dry place.

My coffee was now cold, and the gusting inflow wind had subsided. A more common weather system was now returning to Ocean Falls, the weather it knew best—rain. Watching ERQ pull at its moorings down below that rock wall skirting the road, I became aware of the heavy drops bouncing back from the roadway and the hissing beneath the wheels of the passing trucks and cars as the mill whistle announced the end of shift.

My flying job did not last very long with Ash River and the Kleven family. I received a call from Stan Kaardal, operations manager for Gulf Air in Campbell River. They would be happy to hire me as a line pilot. As Stan continued, he expressed with some amazement that Gulf Air's owner, Don Braithwaite, had no objection to hiring me. Don had been very unhappy with the competition I had given his airline when I was in Shawl Bay and had often expressed what he would like to do to my ass. Stan was amazed that Don had

An earlier photo of the Island Airlines dock at the Campbell River spit. The aircraft on the end of the dock is a collector's item "Husky," with the Leonides 550-horsepower engine conversion done by Dave Nilson. "STONEY" JACKSON PHOTO

recanted. "I guess he would rather have you on side," he ventured.

When I broke the news to the Klevens, they understood the opportunity facing me. A good friend was looking for a flying job, so I recommended to the family that they hire him. Graham Wilson became the company pilot, and both parties enjoyed a long, productive relationship. I joined Gulf Air on March 6, 1980, and was immediately introduced to Bob Pogue. Bob was chief pilot for the company and responsible for all check rides and training flights. He was also a very well known and highly respected coast pilot whose flying abilities were legendary. Somewhat intimidated at first to have such a professional checking my flying skills, I was soon at ease with this

ingenuous and often humorous man.

Bob had a sense of humour and an intellect quite beyond what one would expect to find with bush pilots, but he suffered fools badly and had screwed up his own advancement in the industry by telling some key people where to stick their job. He made a lasting impression on me and was responsible for checking me out on the Beaver and single Otter aircraft of the fleet, which I began flying on the local scheduled flights and charters during that first month with the airline.

Gulf Air's competition at the Campbell River spit was Island Airlines, whose founder, Bob Langdon, had been the first to establish an air service after the demise of what had been the largest seaplane airline in the world, BC Air-

Stan Kaardal, operations manager at Gulf Air when I joined. Stan, who has spent forty-five years as a "coast dog," has more hours on one type of airplane than many have for totals. The last time I spoke to him he was complaining that he no longer liked to fly in quarter-mile visibility.

lines. Gulf and Island were not always friendly in their rivalry, but they co-existed on adjacent docks with only occasional clashes. Langdon always insisted that Don Braithwaite was an upstart. Braithwaite, on the other hand, picked up some of the local business through his many friendships with the loggers in the area.

The intense competition put a strain on Gulf Air's business, and a manager had been appointed. Doreen Bowers was in total control of Gulf Air at the time I joined the company. She was

extremely capable and had an iron grip on Braithwaite's amiable tendency to give away the farm. It was she who had gained the expertise of long-time coastal pilot Stan Kaardal as operations manager and of Bob Pogue as chief pilot.

As I was flying around the coast in those superb Beavers and Otters, enjoying my new life as a commercial pilot, an entrepreneur by name of Jimmy Pattison was buying up all the airlines he could lay his hands on, with the plan of creating a regional service. Under the operative name of the Pattison Group, Air West had been the first to go, followed by Pacific Coastal Airlines and Trans-Provincial Airlines. Then the heat came on next door at Island Air and on Gulf Air to sell out to the Pattison Group. Under Doreen's guidance the deal was consummated, and Don Braithwaite traded his fleet and licences and liabilities for some heavy cash. The same thing happened at Island Air, and the two airlines were integrated.

Nobody was seeking my advice during this period, and I continued to build time and enjoy the life while a succession of general managers of the new company came and went, as Pattison sought out the right man to put this conglomerate on course. I was living in Campbell River during my flying shifts, in a shared basement

105

apartment with Graham Wilson, who was doing my previous job of flying ERQ. My regular schedule established, for the first time in three years, some job security and routine time off for trips home to Qualicum Beach. I was enjoying the stability of this routine.

One bright morning early in November, I returned to work at Campbell River after three days off and was confronted with one of those offers a pilot cannot refuse.

"Jack, have we got a deal for you," Pogue announced in the pilots' lounge.

Single Otter LCP. Wonderful airplanes to fly, the Otter and Beaver are totally different to handle. A Workers' Compensation Board inspector flew up front with me one day and measured the decibel level in the cockpit. He said the noise level was beyond the acceptable level for any workplace. To this I answered, "What did you say?"

"You can take an extended vacation—like forever—or you can accept a transfer up to Port Hardy, where you will fly amphibs off the runway at the airport." Everybody in the lounge was grinning, some more nervously than others because, if I refused the transfer, some other innocent sod would get the same terms. It seems that during my days off the pilots of both Island Air and Gulf Air had been given seniority numbers, and mine was so high up there among the discards that I was lucky to get any consideration at all.

"You get up there in Port Hardy," laughed Pogue, "and they'll forget all about you. You'll have a job forever, maybe make it to president." There was a sigh of relief from some of the other high-number types when I accepted the transfer. "Come with me," said Pogue, gesturing for me to follow him down the stairs to the seaplane dock. "I'm going to check you out on amphibious aircraft." I followed, dutifully, and kept looking for a different airplane on the dock, thinking that an amphib had come down from Port Hardy on which he would give me a check ride.

All the planes were our regular straight-float machines, and when we reached the very end of the dock I was somewhat incredulous as Pogue turned

to me and poked me repeatedly on the clavicle. "There is an old saying about flying amphibs," he said, getting decidedly stern in voice and demeanour, "that there are only two kinds of amphibious pilots—those who have and those who will."

At this point Bob was getting red in the face. He stuck his face close to mine and yelled, "That saying is bullshit! Don't you ever—do you hear me—don't you *ever* leave your wheels in the wrong position." He then stamped off down the dock, leaving me dumbfounded about his checkout on amphibious floats. This bizarre experience did, however, stay with me, and for many years I lived in fear of ever again having to inform Pogue that I had landed in the water with my wheels down or on the runway with my wheels retracted.

I bid my erstwhile colleagues goodbye. The more senior ones were destined for Vancouver, to become the glamour boys for the emerging regional commuter airline, while others were staying on at Campbell River, apprehensive of their futures. The new name of Air BC was now emblazoned on all the aircraft, and our future was, figuratively, tied to that big "A" on our tail.

107

11
YZT AND THE MURAL

On November 18, 1980, I drove up Vancouver Island with an overnight bag and some apprehension. I knew a few things about YZT, as Port Hardy airport was designated, but nothing very current. The airport had been built in 1943 under the supervision of a brilliant, irascible, hard-drinking civil engineer by the name of Gray Margach, under contract to the Department of National Defence. He had been the site engineer for two other major wartime airports located at Abbotsford and Comox. I know this because the man was my mother's brother—my uncle—and "irascible" is a polite description of him.

Armed with a preconception of Port Hardy gained in my youth from hearing this awesome man describe it as "not the rectum of the world but six inches up," I arrived at YZT and was pleasantly surprised to find a modern terminal building and control tower equipped with what appeared to be secondary radar facilities. Its three paved runways, built to handle World War II bombers being staged on to Russia, were more than adequate for the peacetime traffic of one Pacific Western Airlines Boeing 737 a day plus a gaggle of little amphibians. The town of Port Hardy, a few miles down the highway, would be my home away from home for the next two years.

My boss was Villi Douglas, a legendary aviation personality who had been a pilot and dispatcher for the pioneer airline Alert Bay Air Services during the immediate postwar days. The six other pilots working for the company were a mixed bag of great guys; although each has now gone his separate way, a camaraderie still exists between us because of our shared experiences at this base in the north island area. Whenever our paths cross there is that sense of "old home week," and inevitably some of the adventures are paraded out for the enjoyment of retelling.

Six of the pilots at Port Hardy were billeted at the company-owned duplex a few blocks from the airport. This duplex was quite new and adequately appointed, although the furniture had not withstood the ravages of a succession of indifferent pilot-tenants. The company duplex became the focal point for the colourful and varied lifestyles of the young men who were "building time" in their chosen career at Port Hardy. The adage "If the walls could talk" certainly applied to the events that took place here. Probably those who now reside in this building are still uncovering vestiges of the place's history.

The aircraft at Air BC's Port Hardy operation were all amphibious—three Beavers, two single Otters and two Cessna 185s, plus a twin-engine, ten-passenger, wheelplane called a BN2, a Britten Norman Islander. The fleet also sported three Grumman Goose flying boats. These aircraft were all housed in an enormous hangar built during my uncle's reign of terror during World War II. So large was this hangar that it stored all eleven aircraft as well as half-a-dozen private machines and still had enough space left over to house the company's maintenance department.

My first flying duties were performed on the Cessna 185s registered IGJ and CLU. The amphibious gear on a 185 is retracted by an electric motor driving a hydraulic system that tucks the main wheels into the step compartment of the floats and the nose gear into wells located in the pointy end of the pontoons. In addition, the 185 has all sorts of bells and whistles and outside mirrors serving to assure you, among other things, that your gear is retracted or extended. The entire rig adds considerably to the empty weight of the plane and thus reduces the load-carrying ability of the Cessna. A pilot and two passengers is the accepted load for an amphib 185, but if those two passengers are big loggers with an extra pair of boots you'll have some trouble getting airborne.

Of the two 185s, CLU was the better performer, getting off the water faster, carrying bigger loads and cruising faster. It was a doggy-looking plane but a great performer and much preferred by the pilots. Only after a year had passed was it determined that CLU's manifold pressure gauge was under-reading, thus giving more power for the specified throttle and pitch settings. We had been operating the engine beyond its safe limits and had never realized it. After that discovery the engineers recalibrated the instrument, making CLU perform like a dog.

Since the mainland area we served from the base at Port Hardy was well

This single Otter, pictured on the seaplane ramp at Ocean Falls, is QRI still painted in Gulf Air green. It was traditional to stand other pilots a case of beer if you left your water rudders down, but this time no one noticed until the film was developed. BRIAN SCHOFIELD PHOTO

known to me from my Shawl Bay days, a route check was not required. However, I needed a checkout on the amphibious versions of the Beaver and Otter as well as a multi-engine endorsement for the Islander. These training duties were all performed, and soon I was flying all the aircraft types in the fleet except the Goose, for which there were already more pilots than airplanes.

The Port Hardy group included a few colourful characters. One of the pilots was natty; you would never catch him on duty with a hair out of place.

He presented himself with a somewhat Prussian air of efficiency, his erect carriage and steel-grey hair reinforcing that impression and his clipped speech furthering the image. This effect was particularly laid on for the ladies. A dash of distinctive cologne as an aftershave was the man's calling card. Flying an airplane immediately after he had flown it was like stepping into a whore's boudoir; you had to wipe the control yoke and throttle if you didn't want to wear the scent I dubbed Oscar De La Aviateur.

Amphibious Beavers and Otters were the principal aircraft at YZT, with two Cessna 185s also on strength. Fellow-pilot Doug Banks, at the bow of the Beaver float, is telling me war stories as Beaver OCQ is fuelled up. BRIAN SCHOFIELD PHOTO

The camaraderie at Port Hardy was the result of sharing the dangers of flying at the scary speed of ninety-five miles an hour and attending the strip show in town each Monday night—I am not certain which was the more harrowing. I was mutton dressed as lamb, but became as entangled in this bootless lifestyle as the younger pilots. The shared experience of a number of misadventures bound us as comrades forever. One night, for example, one of the ramp attendants fell off his chair down the three steps and onto the stage, where a particularly mature stripper had just cast off her sequined top. She scooped up our favourite ramp rat, who had rolled right to her feet, and jammed his face deep into her ample cleavage. Then she pulled an outsized ten-gallon cowboy hat over all three of them, whereupon the house came down and our young dock boy, absolutely scarlet, returned to the table in total disarray. The stripper, whose advertising pictured her as having appeared on a *Star Trek* episode as a member of an Amazonian spear-carrying tribe, appeared at YZT the next morning with one of our more senior pilots and gained a free ride up the coast, sans cowboy hat and spear.

During these early days at Air BC my old friend, Ed Carder, had been busy at Minstrel Island. Ed had quickly filled the vacuum created in the area when I had folded up my charter service out of Shawl Bay. All my old customers were now being flown by Ed's little red-and-white Cessna, CF-ZSZ, and many hair-raising tales got back to us about how he would fly in any weather and would often arrive home long after dark. Not only had he established a little airline at Minstrel but also a secondary base at Kelsey Bay, where he had set up Bill Kelly and his wife as agents for Minstrel Air.

The Kellys had their home right on the Salmon River, and the seaplane dock was only a stone's throw from their house. Ed had installed a waiting room on the site and had equipped the Kellys with a VHF aircraft-band transceiver for communication to his plane. He had also purchased a steel hangar and was planning to install it at Kelsey, where he planned to do his aircraft maintenance. In addition, Ed had installed a dock at Alert Bay and had appointed a local business couple as the agent for Minstrel Air. Ed had big plans for Minstrel Air; he had determined, correctly, that there was a soft spot in the Air BC monopoly, starting at Kelsey Bay and extending to Port McNeill, where he had also purchased a large

waterfront building suitable for a hangar. He was doing things that had been part of my earlier plan, and I envied him the adventure.

But fate had some bad news for the Carders. Ed's wife, Margit, after returning from a trip to Germany, was diagnosed with brain cancer. Margit spent many weeks in a hospital in Victoria, and Ed dropped his flying to be with her. He now had two airplanes and obviously needed another pilot to fly for him. He was pretty desperate when he called me, one day, at the Air BC office at Port Hardy. Villi Douglas took the call and handed me the phone, explaining that someone from a radio phone wanted to talk to me.

"Jack," said a faint voice, "come to Minstrel and fly for me." Ed explained his plight: he was spending more and more time with Margit in Victoria, and he would like someone to run the airline in his absence. He was devastated when I told him that I felt my future was better with Air BC. I could tell he had banked on convincing me to make the move. When I hung up I told Villi about the call, and he told me David Reaville, the son of a veteran coast pilot now flying for Air BC, was looking for a flying job. I called Ed back and gave him David's number. Ed hired David, which turned out to be the right move—the young pilot fit right into

113

114

the scheme of things and bailed Ed out of a tough spot.

At Port Hardy, although we were conscious of Ed's activities, there was little real concern about the threat from his competition. Air BC at Port Hardy did not service the southern area in which Ed was energetically building his business, because this was traditionally looked after from Campbell River. The Campbell River operation, however, misjudged Ed's capabilities and did not act as a private entrepreneur would. Had fate not had other plans for Ed Carder, he might well have wiped everyone's slate in the area.

One foggy day in October, Ed disappeared, in ZSZ, on a flight from Port McNeill to the head of Knight Inlet. The next morning Villi handed me four large, thick blotters used to pick up oil samples from the water surface. "Take FJQ with these things and go to Minstrel Island. There's an oil slick on the water right in front. Search-and-rescue wants a sample." I walked out to the Beaver, observing, as I taxied for the runway, the search squadron's Labrador and Buffalo holding because of weather in the high country. Once airborne, I was given further instructions to go to Minstrel and then back to Thomas Point in Kingcome Inlet to pick up further samples from another oil slick that had been sighted.

The search for ZSZ was never done adequately because the weather did not give the searchers a break. Al Halliday of Kingcome Inlet was certain that he had heard Ed overhead at Kingcome on his way up the Simm Creek route into Knight Inlet, but by the time this lead was given the search-and-rescue squadron had called off the search and gone home. Ed was never found, but his influence on my life was yet to be played out.

Returning just at dusk from my blotter flight, I let myself into the duplex and was greeted with one hell of a stink—fishy stuff that made your eyes water. I remembered then that it was Kessel's time of the year—herring season! Kjel (pronounced like Shell) Kessel was a much-loved member of the pilot community at YZT. A man of few words, Kjel was a lover of jazz and had a particular affection for the vocal stylings of Sarah Vaughan, whose last name we all enjoyed hearing him pronounce as "Voggin," with his Norwegian inflection on the V. He had his countrymen's taste for pickled herring and what he described as an excellent recipe for pickling the fish.

Each herring season we others in the duplex lost the use of the bathtub as Kessel filled it with brine and herring, adding a touch of this and that to the stinking concoction, and then left it to

percolate for weeks, during which time no one in our side of the duplex could take a bath or shower. The stench in the place was terrible, but the happy Viking was oblivious to our discomfort, savouring the day when he would bite into that fishy succulence. I never did see Kessel eat his pickled herring, but the smell clings to my memory—as I'm sure it does to the porcelain of the tub and the walls of that duplex.

Kessel had an aversion to talking unless it was to answer a question. He carried this trait into the cockpit when he flew. The necessity of gaining taxi and takeoff clearance from the tower or flight service station at YZT prompted about all that this pilot wanted to say.

When he had completed this formality he would hang up his headphones, turn off the radio and proceed with his flight.

Kessel was a "hacker" and would fly in any kind of weather without comment. I once met his airplane virtually head on while tracking the shoreline in visibility that was down to about a quarter mile. Kjel was doing the same thing in the opposite direction, and we each had to take sudden avoidance action to miss having a mid-air collision. Being a voluble type, I called him on the VHF to express my relief, but my words fell on deaf radios; there was no response. Later, in the pilot's lounge, Kessel's heavily accented reply

MINSTREL AIR

to my exclamations was simply, "We must have missed."

It is an unwritten law that a pilot who gets his undercarriage screwed up and lands either with the gear down in the water or the gear up on the runway automatically gets his walking papers. Before my service at Port Hardy, Kjel had landed in Hardy Bay with his gear extended for a previously planned landing at the airport. The single Otter, with five passengers—all fortunately sitting in the back of the plane—went over on its nose and thrashed the water with its prop, but fell back on the floats. All the passengers spoke up for Kjel, indicating that they had made him change his approach from the airport to the water landing at the last minute. This, combined with the popularity of the pilot among management and the negligible damage to the Otter, resulted in the incident being overlooked. Such was not his fortune on the second occasion.

I came home from the last trip of the day to find Kessel dressed for town and shaking hands, saying goodbye to everyone. In the hangar was QRI, his favourite single Otter, but this time with the float skins ripped open from a wheels-up landing on the runway. It was unthinkable that a fine pilot and good guy like Kessel should bite the dust. I made an ass of myself complaining to Villi that an exception should be made in Kessel's case. Then I learned about the first incident, so I shook hands with Kjel and bid him good luck.

My only misadventure with the amphibious undercarriage was less dramatic than Kjel's, but it was in the same airplane. One of our popular points of call for the Port Hardy operation was Bull Harbour, where a coast guard lighthouse station was maintained. The landing here was made inside a lagoon, which provided calm water on the worst of days, and it was here that I had my first experience with a gear-down landing in the water. I had taken off from Port Hardy in a single Otter, QRI, pumping the gear up in the usual manner. The Otter's nose wheels come right over the front of the floats and position themselves very obviously on the float deck, and they were up there on this occasion. Mirrors out on the lift strut, positioned to provide a view of the main wheel on both sides, give the pilot a visual reference for the wheels, and in the cockpit a barber-pole gauge shows the position, up or down. The barber-pole on this airplane never worked, so once I had a "hard handle," indicating that the hydraulic system had gone as far·as it could go, I checked the mirrors once, after takeoff, and was happy that the wheels were up.

As I flew past the mouth of Hardy Bay, a Cessna 180 belonging to my friend Pat Finnerty, of Sullivan Bay, came flying out at about my altitude and started to fly around me, wagging his wings, peeling off, then returning to perform more antics. I waved at him, thinking he was just saying hello, because we hadn't seen each other for many months. A few minutes later, when on final approach for the lagoon, I could see Pat's airplane on the dock at Bull Harbour. Crossing the low shore of the island, one had to maintain sufficient height to clear the telephone lines, then suck the airplane onto the water as close to the shore as possible. When I touched the water, the aircraft slowed down really fast, and I figured I must have bottomed on a sand bar in the reedy shallows. I taxied into the dock and parked behind Finnerty, opened the little pilot door and was greeted with Finnerty's exclamation.

"You've still got horseshoes up your ass, Schofield. Look at your main gear.

I was trying to tell you—didn't you see me buzzing you?" He explained that his radio was not working, so he couldn't call me. I followed his pointing finger and could see, under the water, a big black tire sticking out of the bottom of the pontoon. I couldn't believe it. It was obvious that I had been flying with my head in the cockpit and didn't read his frantic gesturing toward the under-carriage. The hydraulic pressure had leaked during the flight, and the main gear had come down. I was the dummy, with no valid excuse, because a check for a "hard handle" before landing, part of the required check, would have corrected the problem. Fortunately, as I discovered, the single Otter lands nicely with the main gear extended, so I didn't have to face the indignity of telling Bob Pogue that I committed that sin of sins.

Floatplane pilots see themselves as the latter-day bush pilots and do not take kindly to neckties and uniforms. The James Cagney look from *Captains of the Clouds* suited most of the pilots, but Air BC thought otherwise: this new airline had an image to project, and those bush types up in Port Hardy would start looking the part. We were issued magnificent uniforms suitable for flying 747s, in which one could make announcements commencing with "This is your captain speaking." The blue serge suits, replete with wings and four gold bars, were a cut above the job of loading a Beaver or single Otter on a rainswept dock, and our regular customers were underwhelmed with our new, resplendent image.

Lucky Bachen, who operated the post office and fuel dock at Rivers Inlet, was dazzled by my arrival in this gorgeous outfit and immediately dubbed me "the Admiral," a name that stuck no matter what I wore in subsequent years. Despite the company's insistence that we wear these uniforms, the jackets were soon relegated to the baggage compartment. But we all wore out the two pairs of trousers that were provided, performing what is often a dirty flying job.

Air BC was now emerging as a regional carrier, flying the new de Havilland Dash 7 four-engine airliners. It did not need the high-profile, big "A" on the tail of doggy old floatplanes, with the extreme likelihood of messy accidents, marring its hard-earned image. Air BC chose to have us operate under the name of one of the companies it had taken over—Trans-Provincial Airlines, whose base of operations was Prince Rupert. Our airplanes, some of which were still in Gulf Air green, were now repainted red, white and blue, with TPA logos on their flanks. All our paperwork was done on Trans-Provincial ticket stock, even though we were still paid by Air BC.

During the summer of my second season in Port Hardy, Villi Douglas, either because he wanted to get rid of me or simply out of benevolence, said to me one day, "Jack, why don't you buy the old ABAS (Alert Bay Air Services) licence from Air BC and open an outfit in Alert Bay? Air BC has so many licences that it doesn't even know it's got that one. You could get it for a song." The suggestion was made in passing, and although it seemed like a fine idea, it did not become an imperative. The busy summer was upon us, and our flying duties became paramount.

In any case, I was happy flying for the big guy on the coast; dreams of other enterprises were not on my mind. Villi's suggestion did, however, bury itself in a secret place in my brain. One day it might become an interesting possibility, but for now, this "Admiral" was happy to fly under the ubiquitous TPA logo of a dart in a hoop.

When Jimmy Pattison first started Air BC, he was reported to be fairly strait-laced. Villi Douglas, our base manager, was wrestling with this fact, and he was worried. The pilot's lounge was what worried him. If all the exposed breasts from *Playboy* magazine pinned up on the walls of that room were laid end to

YZT AND THE MURAL

end, they would provide a very soft road to Vancouver. Every inch of the wall was covered, and Villi didn't want Jimmy Pattison to be offended.

"Strip the wall," he ordered, and strip it we did, leaving something else bare —the plywood. "That's okay," Villi said, not realizing that the engineers had installed all that unwanted porn art on the hangar wall, where Jimmy Pattison would undoubtedly encounter it during his tour of the base. Well, Jimmy never showed up and the pilot's lounge felt like a construction shack. The engineers just laughed at the idea of giving all those "collector's items" back to the pilots, so what to do?

The room in question measured sixteen feet by ten feet, and without those bare bodies adorning the wall it was pretty blah. It also now echoed rather badly when six or eight guys were in there telling war stories. I got up on a chair one day and drew a picture in the upper-left-hand corner of that wall. It was a scene of a Canso crossing Cape Caution. I then worked in the old Queen Charlotte Airlines emblem, a shield with two war canoes rampant on a field of the letters QCA. Villi liked that idea and suggested I keep going at it. "Do the whole wall. We'll even buy you the oil paints."

I started thinking about it, and from discussions with some of the old-timers

in the area I realized that many pilots had flown out of here just as I was doing now. I felt that they should be remembered; many had gone on to fly airliners, while others had perished, either flying out of here or elsewhere in this unforgiving business. One airline or another had been based here since 1945, and the way this industry worked, as soon as one failed somebody else bought the planes and started all over again with a new name and a new paint job.

Some research revealed the names of all the operators right up to the present, and I sent out inquiries about the names of pilots who had been based out of Port Hardy. As I painted what was going to be a sixteen-foot mural in the pilot's room, the idea caught on at the airport and I was visited by many people who encouraged the concept. Visiting pilots would stop by and give me the names of others, long gone, who used to fly out of Hardy. I hung a list on the wall for people to write on while I was out flying and spent my spare time sketching the scenes and then scaling them up for transfer to the wall.

My sketches were okay, because I have always been a nut about drawing and have worked in India ink, but I was no painter, and it took a lot of trial and error to learn how to grey the colours and work out different hues. The names

120

were lettered in with a waterproof felt pen. As the wall started to take shape, Villi encouraged me while a long-time local pilot, John Paterson, provided a steady supply of names to add to the growing list.

The mural was to be a series of airplane scenes depicting the resident airlines and highlighting their logos. The names of pilots would be worked in between these scenes, in a break through the painted overcast. It would take a long time because we were flying every day during the summer months and I was playing my trumpet in a dance band in the evenings in preparation for a community concert. Things were great in the flying and performing arts department at Port Hardy that year.

With the passing of the summer months and the heavy flying duties behind us, it was traditional for the airline to lay off all but a few pilots, who were the senior men on the line. I would have suffered this fate too, except that Villi had decided he wanted that mural finished. He made me another one of those deals I couldn't refuse.

"I'll give you the daily mileage of the highest-time pilot," he said, "but you stay right in here and fly that wall." This meant I would be paid my base salary of twelve hundred and fifty dollars plus fourteen cents a mile for the number of miles flown, daily, by the highest-time pilot of each day. I was going to make more money painting this mural than flying airplanes, so it was a deal. I set in to complete the job, working days and often during the evenings until the wee hours of the morning, emulating the lifestyle if not the artistry of the masters.

The mural was completed in December 1981. It depicted the history of the Port Hardy airport in terms of the operators from 1945 to the present and with about two hundred pilots' names, representing those who had been based at this airport over those years. It is not a great work of art, but the mural illustrates the history of the place, and even though I would have liked to do it again with more skill, I was happy to put down the brushes and pick up the airplanes again.

I went home for Christmas on the December 19 and returned a week later to find the mural gone. In its place was a bare plywood wall, painted green like every other Transport Canada wall in the building. This amazing disappearance was soon explained by the new airport manager, who had taken on his duties during the Christmas vacation. Upon seeing the wall, he had it cut out of the pilot's room and mounted in the main public terminal, over the baggage carousel, where it resides to this day.

Doc Pickup

While performing the day-to-day job of flying people and freight around the mid-coast and the north island area, one was ever-conscious of the presence of certain pillars of society—people like the Native chiefs from the three villages, the mayors and council members of Port Hardy, Port McNeill and Alert Bay, the big-business operators of grocery and department stores, the government forestry officials—the movers and shakers of the area. Of all these local leaders, no one's activities were of a higher profile than those of Jack Pickup—"Doc Pickup" to everybody within an area of some eight thousand square miles.

One of the first things Jack Pickup did when he moved into the area in 1947 was to steal the fifty-two-bed hospital from Port Hardy and barge it down to his favourite place, Alert Bay. He didn't really steal it, because the government thought it was a great idea and sold it to the village. Nobody at Port Hardy could have given a damn, in those days, about that wartime air force hospital—good riddance to what was thought to be a hastily built, wooden-framed barrack block.

It took sixteen barges to move Saint George's Hospital onto site at Alert Bay, but when in place it became the centre of the universe for every Native village and logging operation on the mid-coast. Much later, when other doctors took up practice in Port Hardy and Port McNeill, there was no little chagrin that the only hospital in the area was over at Alert Bay—"On an island, would you believe?"

The other thing this young doctor did when he came into the area was go back to Vancouver, learn to fly, get his licence, buy an airplane, fly it back—all in three weeks. Jack Pickup became an instant flying doctor and was soon buzzing around his territory, tending to the sick and injured in their own floating homes or flying out the injured from the logging camps.

Jack started his flying with a Piper Super Cub on floats, but soon moved up to a

Previous page: The
cabin Waco on call
at Shawl Bay, circa
1950.

bigger aircraft. He bought a classic Waco cabin monoplane and became the envy of
airplane buffs everywhere. The Waco required considerable maintenance, and while it
was in Pitt Meadows for repairs Jack used an amphibious Seabee aircraft, which he
liked because he could land it on the dirt strip at Alert Bay or taxi it up onto the
beach. "I found it a lot better for my purposes," Jack once told me. So, he left the
Waco in town and flew the little pusher flying boat around the coast.

124

The doctor, despite being something of a novice pilot, performed some outstanding flying feats during these early days of his practice. Villi Douglas, long-time pilot
and airline operator in the area, told of one incident: "Jack got a call saying that
the lighthouse keeper at Pine Island had taken very sick—could somebody come and
get him? Well, "somebody," in the shape of Jack Pickup and his "Bee," took off in the
teeth of a storm and landed in the open water beside Pine Island, a terrible place on
any day, with big rollers threatening the little airplane.

Somehow he got the plane onto the water without losing it, somehow the patient
was lowered to the beach in a breeches buoy and somehow they got the sick man
into Jack's plane. The big "somehow" was how he managed to get that little under-
powered crate off the water without being swamped by the swells and the crosswind,
but he did it and he got the patient to hospital. "We used to shake our heads at
some of the things he did," laughed Douglas, who had, himself, been a pilot and
dispatcher for the early local airline ABAS (Alert Bay Air Services) during those years.

Jack's flying days tapered off as the hospital demanded more and more of his
attention. There were a couple of local airlines around to call for medivac work, so
more often than not, he left the flying to them and worked his regular twelve-hour
days at the hospital, living only a few yards from the building and constantly on call.

Jack was an extremely innovative man and a gold-medallist graduate from medical
school. Had he set up shop in Vancouver's posh Shaughnessy district he could have
spent half his days on the golf course and be a wealthy man to boot, but Jack figured he was needed here on the coast, and secretly, like the rest of us, he got a real
kick out of flying around this place. Unlike the Shaughnessy doctors, he often took
payment for his services in promises or Native carvings and had a great collection of
the former in his memory and of the latter on the walls of his home.

To unwind from his busy days, Jack would come home and sit down at the piano.
He was a fine jazz pianist, not just good, but professional. "I had to choose between
medicine and music at one point," he told me. "And I often wonder if I made the
right choice," he laughed.

One had to watch Jack Pickup; he had a dry sense of humour and never even twitched when he was pulling your leg. I played along with him on my horn at the Legion one night, and Doc was truly a great jazz musician. He stopped in the middle of one piece, laughing at the recollection of an aircraft engineer known to us both, who played the drums with him and other aviator-musicians long ago. "He was sure a great aircraft engineer," laughed Pickup, continuing with the music.

Jack had a respected reputation as a doctor and humanitarian, but his reputation did not go unscathed in the forty-five years of unstinting service he gave to this area. The criticisms levelled at him in later years were to the effect that he was drinking too much or that he worked such long hours that a man of his age, etc. etc. The principal complaint was that of other doctors attempting to start up a practice in Alert Bay. "I can't get past St. George and the dragon," complained one aspiring M.D., referring to Jack and his principal support team, his wife, Lilla, who held the administration post at the hospital and stood behind this energetic man for all of those forty-five years.

Jack obviously heard and ignored these complaints, and he soldiered on until September 26, 1992. He had, by this time, donated his old Waco cabin monoplane to the aviation museum and announced his formal retirement. The sendoff given Doc Pickup by the village and his hundreds of friends was overwhelming. He moved to Coquitlam on the Lower Mainland, where he passed away a few years later.

If you fly into Alert Bay and land at the airport, your tires will bark on an asphalt runway. When you have parked and got out of your airplane, you will see a stone cairn with a bronze plaque explaining that you have landed on the H. J. Pickup Airfield. Don't wait for Jack; the likes of him will not pass this way again.

12

IF "IFS" AND "ANDS" WERE POTS AND PANS, TINKERS WOULD RIDE

From a sandy hook that forms the little marina called Deep Bay, halfway up the east coast of Vancouver Island, occupants of the houses surrounding the bay look onto the commercial fishing docks from their living-room windows and out to Chrome Island lighthouse and Hornby Island from their kitchens. They probably would not have noticed the Beaver aircraft landing on the outside channel had not their dishes rattled on the shelf and the window glass trembled in its frame. Through the venetian blinds of successive kitchen windows, momentary glimpses of a white aircraft revealed orange wing tips, a blue band halfway along each wing, the name "Air BC" on the fuselage and a big "A," in orange, on the tail.

The third house from the end of the spit viewed the aircraft touching the water and coming off the step in a spray of foam. The water rudders came down, and wallowing from its own landing wake, the plane taxied around

the end of the sandy spit into the bay. The occupants of the last house, who were dining out on their deck, waved to the airplane and observed it on its journey, dividing their attention from the meal at hand to the movement of the plane. There was a sudden quiet in the bay as the aircraft's propeller windmilled to a stop. The seaplane glided, silently, to the dock. The diners resumed their meal, unaware that they had witnessed the first landing of the most recently formed B.C. coastal airline—Orca Air.

"How come the name isn't painted on the plane?" It was my son Brian, asking the most obvious question as we tied off the Beaver for the night and proceeded down the wharf.

"We can't operate as Orca Air until the transfer of the licence is approved by Ottawa," I replied, hoping that he wouldn't ask, "How come?"

He didn't ask, but my other son, Peter, did, and I went into a long,

127

convoluted explanation of how an august body of non-aviation people, appointed by government, ruled on such things. "They take a year to study the matter before we can put our name on the plane," I explained to the incredulous youngsters. "In the meantime, we fly just as if we were Air BC, from whom we bought the airplane and the licence." The boys, too young to spell "bureaucracy" and too polite to say "screw-up," were sorry they asked.

Orca Air was the consummation of all my plans to create a coastal airline operating in the area that I knew so well and that I had abandoned after the crash of XRK. The licence to operate was the very certificate Villi Douglas had once suggested would be available from the newly created Air BC. "They won't even know they've got it," Villi had said, and he was right. Dennis Mercier, searching through the many licences acquired from the takeover of seven coastal airlines, had trouble locating the air-carrier permit, but he finally found it.

I looked over the three Beavers that Air BC had for sale and picked the best one, C-FRQW. John Hill, an independent engineer, did a survey of the plane and gave it a clean bill of health. Orca Air was now in business, and it was, unquestionably, the coastal airline most likely to succeed. We also had the best possible aircraft for the job. Something

else we had, which I had never wanted, was "we" instead of "me."

There must be partnerships that work, but I had not experienced one so far. I had not planned to involve anyone else in what I considered as the blue-chip venture of my lifetime. However, my wife, once bitten, was twice shy and had balked at the financial risk. She would not permit our jointly owned property to be used as collateral for the entire $85,000 investment for the purchase of the plane and licence. She agreed to a one-fifth involvement, leaving me with $5,000 in cash and an agreement permitting only a $30,000 lien against our property (which the bank had valued at $200,000). The bank wanted $25,000 up front as a down payment, and collateral for the $60,000 balance. I was forced to find the additional investment from other partners. No matter how I sliced it, I would now become a minority shareholder in my own airline. I should have taken a paper route, but the desire to keep flying prevailed over good sense.

That businesslike white Beaver, RQW, taxied out of Deep Bay the next morning and, once clear of the populated area, took off on a heading for Alert Bay. The 20 percent owner-pilot at the controls was certain of the new venture's success, but even his innate optimism would not come close to guessing the first year's achievements of Orca Air. He was not to know, as he cleared through the Comox military zone this lovely September morning in 1982, that he would fly this airplane over 800 revenue hours on charter and scheduled flights, that he would fly an additional 273 hours on another leased craft and that he would employ two other pilots and seriously consider the purchase of a second airplane before the end of the airline's fiscal year. He would have smiled broadly had he anticipated the figures put forward at the first annual meeting following the financial report: $330,000 gross revenue, $54,000 profit and an unavoidable tax bill of $13,000.

This, from one-and-a-half airplanes operating from Alert Bay. The shareholders were all delighted, and a letter from the bank commending our rapid paydown rate on the loan was proudly read out to all concerned. The partners in the new success story had not been chosen wisely, but rather with expedience. The Alert Bay couple were the people appointed by Ed Carder for his dispatch service and with whom I had worked for less than a month. They had quickly volunteered to come up with $5,000 each when I spoke of forming an airline and required more capital. They also had close friends in Port McNeill, they said, Mrs. Gilbert

and her son, who also came up with $5,000 apiece. In addition, these investors were to provide the balance of the required collateral for the loan to the bank's satisfaction. The sad part was that either one of these family groups outvoted me two to one, and together they represented 80 percent of the stock. I was just the fat boy in the corner with a good idea, a knowledge of the market and the ability to go out and get it.

The other galling facts were that I was the only aviation person in the group and had all the business contacts from my previous years in the area. I had played smart on only one thing: I insisted on a salary for acting as chief pilot and on another for acting as operations manager. The combination, totalling $3,000 per month, was an excellent salary in those days. Howard and Twinkle, from Alert Bay, became the working shareholders of the airline. Howard handled the radio dispatch from the airport terminal building, which was rented from the village of Alert Bay. From this high point on the island we enjoyed excellent radio communication to the plane. Howard's voice could pierce the ether without benefit of radio, so when he barked into my headphones that I had three out of Gilford, two out of Shoal Harbour and groceries on the dock for Kingcome, I would have to either crank down the volume or slip one headphone up off my ear.

Twinkle handled the telephone bookings while Howard pivoted around in a huge, black executive chair that he had purchased as a statement of his importance. Howard had a temper, but I liked the guy. He worked hard and put in as long hours as I did. He lugged an awful lot of groceries down to the seaplane dock during the day, ran passengers around and helped load the plane when he wasn't swivelling in his chair and barking at me in the plane. He could be quite buoyant when in a good humour, and we worked well together, despite the fact that he often left me smoking with anger.

When Twinkle spelled off Howard at the dispatch job, things would calm down. She was equally efficient but not so tempestuous, so she was easier to work with.

"Every morning, I fly over to Port McNeill to pick up our first load of passengers. If we have the two planes operating, both of them fly over there. We're in and out of there all day. We should be based in Port McNeill." I was addressing a shareholders' meeting. "No," said Twinkle. "No," Howard echoed. Although they were willing to admit that we were getting most of our business from Port McNeill, the two Alert Bay shareholders were not prepared to move the airline. "Maybe someday," said Howard, "but not yet." The two Gilbert family shareholders agreed with my proposal, resulting in a majority decision to move, but we didn't want to ramrod the decision. The proposal was shelved until the next meeting.

Port McNeill is thirty-five road miles from Port Hardy, where Air BC was operating with amphibious airplanes from the airport. Loggers and tourists with destinations on the mainland were happy to turn off at Port McNeill, save themselves some extra driving and fly from a location that reduced the air miles and the cost. We had developed regular scheduled flights out of McNeill, and several falling contractors and contract logging companies were using us. We were flying back-to-back, full-load scheduled flights out of McNeill as much as six times a day, every day, to one or another of fifty-two approved stops on the mainland, and we were refuelling at Sullivan Bay, the only source of avgas. This was a very cumbersome arrangement, adding extra costs as a result of deadheading to and from Alert Bay and sometimes Sullivan Bay for fuel. Although the move to McNeill was to be delayed, we agreed to equip an old pickup truck

130

belonging to the Gilberts as a fuel truck and to fuel up in Port McNeill.

"Good God, the brakes don't work on this thing!" I cried as the old truck careened down the long, steep hill into the townsite of Port McNeill on my first fuelling trip. I had three hundred imperial gallons of aviation fuel in two tanks in the back of the clapped-out Chevy. That's twenty-one hundred pounds, I thought, as I wrestled with the swiftly accelerating vehicle. The weight in the box was making the pickup so light on the front wheels that I couldn't stop the thing. I had visions of plunging through the buildings and becoming a headline: "Local Aviator Becomes Fireball." But I managed to stop those printing presses and the truck before disaster struck, and performed our first refuelling at Port McNeill.

The operation was a fire marshal's nightmare: we ran three hundred feet of farm-grade rubber hose down the streets of the town, over the rip-rap of the breakwater and into the Beaver, which was nosed onto the jagged rocks below. A perceptive member of the town council watched me perform this procedure and later that day appeared with a beautiful dock, which he gave to us for our exclusive use for passenger pickups and refuelling. While securing the dock in place, he launched into a scathing attack on his fellow council-men and the local merchants for not recognizing that Orca Air was bringing big bucks into the town.

"You guys deserve some special attention," stormed Graham McDonald. He must have awakened city hall on his next visit, for we were soon made very welcome by the mayor and the business community. Gerry Furney, the long-time mayor of Port McNeill, told me many years later that he didn't then believe that an airline could survive in Port McNeill.

A few days later, I taxied into Sullivan Bay to explain to my friends, Pat and Lynn, why we weren't buying gas from them. During my explanation, I became uncomfortable. They weren't taking it all that well. This surprised me, because gas sales had never been a big item with them. When I had finished my little story, Lynn spoke up. "It would be nice if you paid your bill here, Jack," she said, rather tersely. I was dumbfounded. "Our bill? Do we owe you something?"

"Thirty-six thousand dollars," Lynn replied, extending a sheaf of fuel slips toward me. I was speechless. Howard and Twinkle were the appointed book-keepers, charged with paying all the bills, and we had no reason to complain —everything was paid right up, I thought. Our cash flow was outstanding, and there was no reason for not

paying our gas bill each month. This volume of fuel would represent about five to six months' flying. I took off, assuring my friends that I would be back with an explanation.

"They didn't pick up their mail. It happened two months in a row, so we just stopped sending their cheque," said Twinkle, explaining why the fuel bills had not been paid. Lynn and Pat had gone home for the winter, leaving me with access to the pumps on the honour system. I had left a copy of each fuel sales slip on the clipboard at Sullivan Bay and turned one in to our office. The cheques were sent to Sullivan Bay, where they remained in the mail sacks, uncashed.

Although it was an oversight that Lynn hadn't given winter mailing instructions, I knew the address at Cortes Island where Pat and Lynn wintered and could have dealt with the problem. An account could have been set up to hold the money, but instead we had just not paid them and were now in trouble. There was no question

RQW, our flagship Beaver, in Air BC paint. We were required to fly her for a year under the Air BC name. After a few months of this complicated procedure, Air BC president Iain Harris balked at the complications and told us to put our own name on it and "send back the ticket stock." Too busy to stop for paint, we cut a stencil and slapped it on top of the Air BC logo—Orca Air was born. BRIAN SCHOFIELD PHOTO

of wrongdoing here, but I thought it had been handled very badly. I felt like a thief, taking advantage of good friends. Orca Air was unable to come up with that much cash all at once and had to pay it down over three months of flying.

There were a few shareholder donnybrooks over the handling of this matter, and some enmity developed between the Alert Bay delegation and the three shareholders favouring the move to Port McNeill. At the next shareholders' meeting we voted on the matter, and not surprisingly, three voted in favour and two vehemently against. Amid much dissension, we decided to move the airline to Port McNeill.

The day following our stormy meeting, another pilot and I went over to Alert Bay and flew the planes to Port McNeill. The Port McNeill partners and I were employing a pilot by this time and had leased a beautifully restored Beaver, C-FJOM, from an old friend, Al Beaulieu, of Pacific Aircraft Salvage in Vancouver. Orca's Alert Bay partners were still furious, but we figured they would soon cool down and come back aboard, if only to protect their respective investments.

The two Beavers were now flying out of Port McNeill with great success. Loggers, fallers, tourists, fishermen, residents of the three Native villages,

the provincial health nurse, the doctors' run and provincial flight warrants were keeping both planes in the air full time. The two planes were now manned by three pilots, which divided the flying time equitably and safely between "Super Dave" Kopak (as he was known to his female admirers), Bill Truttman and myself. Both Dave and Bill were PWA pilots sweating out a temporary layoff resulting from an airline strike. They were both great, dependable pilots and good people to have around.

Although Orca Air prospered, we three remaining shareholders were served a summons to defend ourselves in the B.C. Supreme Court for having moved the airline to Port McNeill. Before any conclusive decision was made, however, fate played a wild card. It was December 23, 1983, and many residents of Kingcome village had ordered their Christmas groceries from the Shoprite store in Port McNeill. These orders included Christmas turkeys, which were eagerly expected at the village. In addition, Whonnock Forest Products had twenty-odd turkeys on hand for their employees at the Kingcome camp. All these Christmas supplies arrived at our office in Port McNeill too late in the afternoon to be flown in on that day. Since all our pilots had gone home for Christmas, I decided to fly the grocery run early the next

133

morning. JOM was readied for the nine hundred pounds of freight by removing all the seats except the pilot's to make room for the many boxes. I planned to fly these groceries in to camp the next morning and then shut down the airline for the Christmas holidays.

At seven o'clock the following morning I taxied off the dock with the freight load. Before I had taxied back to what we referred to as the "corner" of the bay, from where we started our takeoff run, I noted that the huge dredge that had been dredging the bay and building a new breakwater was still at work, close to the shore and near the marina. I wondered, as I took off, how long it would be before the dredge completed its work in the harbour, because it had been dredging here for several weeks. Port McNeill harbour is a cranky place to operate a seaplane. In a southeast wind, one performs the takeoff or landing with a thirty-degree crosswind. If an aircraft doesn't get airborne before the breakwater, the huge waves in the outer harbour area could swamp it and will certainly make the pilot abort his takeoff. The thirty-degree crosswind also becomes critical when the wind speed is high.

We had perfected a takeoff and landing procedure that worked well for us and used the Beaver's excellent STOL (short take-off and landing) features to great advantage. There was a moderate gusty southeast wind when I left McNeill, destined for Kingcome village with the groceries. Arriving at Kingcome twenty minutes later, I found that the flying conditions were idyllic. I buzzed the village soccer field and saw two men wave back as they headed for their boats to meet me at the dock in the lower reaches of the river. Later, with the groceries gone and the plane very light due to the absence of the seats, I landed at Sullivan Bay and gassed up all three tanks to make JOM ready for the Boxing Day rush we were expecting after Christmas.

When I returned to Port McNeill I was greeted with a distressing revelation. The McKenzie Barge and Derrick crew had anchored their huge dredge right in the middle of the landing area—a registered airport—and had gone home for Christmas. There was room to land beside the barge, but I would be sixty degrees out of wind and the southeasterly wind was now snorting with strong gusts. I figured the barge provided an excellent windbreak, noticing that the water was slick on the lee side of the big craft. I never doubted that I was a good enough pilot to put JOM onto the water beside the dredge and be off the step before I emerged from the safety of this windbreak. I would later learn that this was my nine

134

hundred and sixtieth landing at Port McNeill, and it proved to be the one that got away.

JOM came off the step a little later than planned and emerged out of the safe area at a fair speed. Now in heavy water, the left float went down into a trough, causing the right wing to rise. One powerful gust came from the direction of the marina broadside against the aircraft, catching that upgoing wing. The left wing buried its tip and JOM went over, nose first, onto her back, as in slow motion, filling the cabin with gasoline-laden water. In sheer disbelief, I had unlatched the pilot door as she was rolling, and I watched the door slide off its hinges and slip into the depths.

As JOM became totally submerged, now suspended beneath her still-buoyant pontoons, the seat belt on the pilot seat whipped itself around my leg and held fast. I had to go back into the cabin, breathing from a bubble of air at the windshield, to dislodge the belt before climbing out onto the spreader bars between the floats.

There is no point in saying how I felt. This was the prettiest airplane I had ever flown, and it was the flagship of Orca Air, complete with our snappy killer-whale motif on her flank. I had sunk her by my own stupid miscalculation. I should have aborted the landing

and gone up to Hardy Bay and taken a taxi home for Christmas. As it was, I spent Christmas Eve wrapped up in the local hospital with a thermometer stuck into a most unlikely place, fighting hypothermia.

The indignity of performing like this right in the harbour, where everyone in town could see the proud local airline take a bath, was mortifying. Adding salt to the wound, three Port McNeill kids that Christmas received T-shirts bearing the slogan "Fly with Snorkel Air."

Fate was still dealing from the bottom of the deck. On December 31— New Year's Eve and one week later, RQW was preparing to depart with three passengers aboard and a fair jag of freight. I was about to handle the plane off the dock when a well-known customer came running down the ramp with one of those huge hardshell suitcases you buy at Canadian Tire. "Wait for me," he shouted, "I'm going to Kingcome." Doug Brown, who was flying RQW, looked a little askance because he figured he had his load, but our friend started to climb aboard, having spotted the one empty seat. I offered to fly him in later if he would wait, but he was already aboard. "This is fine, Jack. I'll just keep my luggage right here on the floor in front of me."

Doug shrugged an "okay" and I closed the door on them, reminding our

The *Vancouver Sun*, December 13, 1982: the notice of transfer of commercial service from Air BC to Orca Air. It took a year for the transfer to become official.

late arrival to do up his seat belt. RQW taxied out toward "the corner" as I turned to chat with a fisherman friend who had come alongside the seaplane dock in his troller. With his engine still running, the fisherman started to apologize for using the seaplane dock, explaining that he was planning to be here for a only few minutes. The roar of RQW in takeoff drowned out his further comments and I looked up to see the Beaver, not yet airborne and fast approaching the huge waves of the outer waters. There was a sharp crack as the plane struck the first big wave. It jumped into the air, perhaps some sixty feet, engine roaring at high boost, straining to stay there. In silhouette against the late afternoon overcast I can see it yet as it rolled onto its side in mid-air, then crashed into the water and disappeared.

I stepped into the boat, that cold hand of desperate fear gripping my guts. Without a word, my fisherman friend cast off and powered, at full throttle, to the scene of the crash. There was nothing on the water—no airplane, no wreckage, no people. Suddenly, as we approached, a head popped up, followed by another, then two more, and finally pilot Doug Brown surfaced. A few bits and pieces floated by, including a dead cat, the pet of a young passenger.

The boat stopped among the struggling survivors. I reached down and grabbed Mrs. Smith, and I got Don, her husband, by the belt and pulled them both to the boat. Don clung to the chine strip as I attempted to get his wife aboard. She proved too heavy for me to lift up over the three feet of the ship's gunwale, so I dragged her astern and pulled her, with a superhuman strength coming to me from somewhere within that dreadful icy panic, over the stern and into the boat. In the process, her clothing caught on the stern controls and the engine went into full power ahead, until it was stopped by the skipper. He then was forced to power the ship in reverse into the swimming people, who were now reacting to the icy water and would soon founder if we didn't get them aboard.

The late-arriving passenger swung himself out of the water, over the rail and into the ship, and started to help me wrestle Don Smith aboard. Don was followed by his young daughter, who was lamenting the loss of her cat. Last aboard was Doug Brown, who was totally fatigued from having dived down to open the cabin door, which the passengers had been unable to do.

The fear, panic and confusion, in addition to the fact that the huge suitcase and other freight had lodged in the cabin area when the plane slammed

On the dock at King-come. The Beaver in the foreground is IPL, owned by Whonnock Forest Products, and Orca's AQX is behind. Kingcome was a regular call for Orca Air.

into the water, had made escape nearly impossible. Doug had reached into the cabin, grabbed somebody by the foot and yarded him out of the sunken plane; he again pulled someone out of the cabin and the little girl emerged on her own. Totally exhausted, he had taken on a lot of water and had developed a terrible yellow colour to his skin

as we dragged him aboard and motored back to the now-waiting ambulance at the government dock.

RQW had gone to the bottom instantly and lay in thirty feet of frigid water. Doug told me later that the front float strut had snapped when the plane hit the first wave. The right-hand float cocked upward and was cut off by the whirling propeller. When RQW hit the water on her side, the remaining pontoon was wrenched off the plane from the impact and the hull went down like a stone. The loose float disappeared and was, apparently, never found. All the passengers were uninjured, although Don Smith suffered terrible shock. He told me that he had accepted the fact that he was about to die and, being a religious man, had commenced making peace with his maker when somebody pulled him out of the plane by his foot.

When I finally got home that night I stripped off my soaking clothes to reveal my upper body, completely black and blue, bruised from that strength I had found in the cold fear that gripped me when I thought those passengers might be lost.

After the shock, after the agony of seeing our wrecked Beaver come out of the depths, came the restructuring of the airline. It didn't, however, prove to be all that difficult, and despite losing our entire fleet in one week we were back in business almost immediately with a leased Beaver from Trevor Ross, of Vancouver. This airplane, MGD, was another one of Al Beaulieu's great-looking rebuilds.

Although we had suffered a very bad blow, a stroke of good fortune occurred to save us from total loss. One week before Christmas and before our first

accident, the Canadian Transport Commission had sent a letter to Air BC announcing the official transfer of the licence to Orca Air. Air BC had not yet removed our airplanes from its fleet insurance policy. As a newly licensed carrier we were required to apply for an operating certificate from Transport Canada, which involved considerable paperwork and a physical inspection of our aircraft, facilities and operating methods. During the period of this application we were forced to shut down the airline. Had Air BC not been so busy, it would have struck our aircraft off the insurance immediately, and our two accidents would not have been covered.

Our two pilots returned home, crashed out of a job, and I started to fly all the trips again. The new Beaver was soon earning its keep. I wanted to purchase the craft from Trevor Ross, but the articles of our company required all the partners' approval for such an acquisition, and unanimity didn't exist. Trevor sold the plane to an interior operator, so we were forced to return it at the end of October 1984. By this time, the airline was back on its feet again and business was looking good, but the situation with the partnership had to be solved before we could expand. I thought I might have a solution.

An American Vietnam vet who was living in the area had made it known to me, on several occasions, that he would like to buy into the airline. He was a former jet jockey, having been blown out of the sky by a SAM missile during the early days of that war. Spike, as he introduced himself, had been an inmate of the "Hanoi Hilton," as the Viet Cong prison was known, for seven years. He was listed as dead by the U.S. military but resurrected during the peace talks as a bargaining piece by the Viet Cong. He was an extremely colourful guy and had more than a few bucks to spend on an airline. In addition, he had his own Cessna 185 floatplane. The thought of having another pilot as a partner and getting out of this bloody mess appealed to me. It seemed to be the only solution, so I had a proposal for him: "If you can get those people over in Alert Bay to sell their stock, I'll buy out the Gilberts. You and I will then be fifty-fifty in the airline."

A week went by, and damned if Spike didn't show up again, stating that he had bought out those shares in the company from our Alert Bay partners. He also threw a curve by arriving with another partner, one Gordon Baird, who had recently acquired Minstrel Island Resort, and who had, presumably, picked up half of those Orca shares and was now to be an equal, one-third partner in the airline. I did not like this turn of events, because in a

three-way partnership it took only two shareholders to gang up on one and run him out of the company.

My personal life was undergoing a major revamp at this time and I was fast having enough of this backroom–boardroom crap—it was taking the fun out of flying. We had been leasing AQX, a Beaver owned by Blair McLean, a sportfishing tycoon from Campbell River. He had warned us that it would be a short-term lease, because he wished to sell the airplane. Under the circumstances, the only person who had the bucks to buy it was Spike, and this fact was used as ammunition by him and Gordon Baird when they laid the heavy on me to take me out of the picture. "If you don't step out, I'm going to take my airplanes and go home," was the convincing sales pitch that gave me back my original five-grand investment and a one-way trip down the highway. Gordon Baird also transferred his shares to Spike immediately following my demise, and a year later Spike sold the airline to Tom Langdon.

"Well, at least you created a lot of employment income, lots of cash flow, aircraft sales, lease payments, investment income, bank interest and gasoline sales." That was my wiseacre brother's take on the entire affair. I had to admit it just about summed up my blue-chip venture of a lifetime.

13

SHOOTING THE MESSENGER AND OTHER WAR STORIES

Gord Jenkins and I used to honk as we passed each other, in the early morning, on our ways to work. He was driving from Port Hardy to Port McNeill to fly for Orca Air, now owned by Spike; I was travelling from Port McNeill to Port Hardy to fly for Trans-Provincial Airlines, the new name on the old Air BC fleet. Forty-five minutes after Spike had fired me, I was hired by Trans-Provincial Airlines, one of the companies, based in Prince Rupert, that Jimmy Pattison had bought out during Air BC's formation—a fact not apparent to the travelling public.

I was back with my old mural, flying the same Beavers, Otters and Islanders that once bore the names of Gulf Air and Air BC and that I had flown six years before. Clayton Hutchings was the new base manager at Port Hardy; Villi Douglas had moved to Vancouver as vice-president in charge of special services for the new regional airline. Clayton was a Newfoundlander with a

lot of bush experience throughout Canada.

It was a pleasure to be on amphibs again and to fly the single Otter and Islander from the convenience of the airport, but driving to and from Port McNeill each day was a pain. This, coupled with the letdown of being a line pilot for somebody else after running my own show, took its toll. Could this be boredom? I would never have admitted it, but, in retrospect, the year was pleasant—perhaps bland—and not marked with significant adventures. This situation lasted for exactly one year, from August 1985 until the same month in 1986, when I took my leave from TPA. I had enjoyed the companionship of the pilots and the familiarity of the mid-coast area we served, but I was now ready for the down-island move long planned with my new "significant other." We took up residence in Parksville, and I sought out a flying job in the area.

I found Tom and Linda Baxter at

Nanaimo, operating an airline called Thunderbird Air. They employed me to fly one of their cream-puff Beavers back and forth between downtown Nanaimo and Vancouver harbour. From within the clique of airline operators working the Vancouver area in 1985, the year the Baxters started Thunderbird Air, something close to disdain was extended to any country yokel with the temerity to invade the most competitive aviation market in B.C. The attrition rate for would-be airlines was higher here than in any place on the coast. It followed that fledgling Thunderbird Air would become just another name on the list of the fallen. Tom Baxter, however, was not a pilot who wanted to become a businessman; he was a businessman turning himself into a pilot, and his invasion of the local market with his one airplane had outstanding and long-lasting results.

The Baxters had initially come to Nanaimo simply as visitors. They were taken with the idea of operating an airline out of Nanaimo's beautiful harbour and decided to stay. Tom had been a building contractor in Kelowna and flew his own Cessna 180 seaplane. He and Linda were practised at being a close-working business team, and they shared a love for airplanes. They started up by offering scenic flights of the local area while seeking investment capital to set up a scheduled service from downtown Nanaimo to downtown Vancouver. They found their capital from an investment group, who backed the airline in exchange for a 60 percent equity in the business. This got Tom into some heavier iron than his little Cessna, and he rejuvenated an old idea: harbour-to-harbour air service.

It's an old saw that timing is everything, but Tom Baxter also brought good business sense into play when establishing his Nanaimo-to-Vancouver service. Instead of using an airliner concept, with a big plane like a twin Otter on floats, which had already been tried, he used several de Havilland Beavers, gussied up to suit the clientele. Offering seven flights per day in both directions, Baxter's service appealed to salespeople, lawyers, doctors and other professional people wanting to hit the big city for a day, do their business and then get home again. The return fare was a much better deal than paying for a hotel room in either city, and landing in the downtown area of each city put Tom's passengers right on target. If more than six people showed up for a flight, Tom would run a second section with another cream-puff Beaver.

I joined Thunderbird Air early in March 1988 as a line pilot, carving a groove in both directions at eight hundred feet on the twenty-five minute

142

flights back and forth between the two cities for the next fourteen months. It was certainly a different flying scene from the one I had been used to. The trade-off was lawyers for loggers, and it didn't take long to realize which were the more interesting.

During these months, Baxter had two Beavers of his own and one leased machine, as well as two Cessna 185s for charter work. The success of the concept had been well established before I came along, and we had good loads in both directions for most of the seven daily flights. On those occasions when only one or two people travelled, Baxter could congratulate himself that he wasn't flying a twin Otter. Although nothing spectacular took place during

One of "Baxter's Beavers" on the dock at the Nanaimo seaplane base. The terminal building at Nanaimo is the finest facility on the coast, boasting a fine restaurant and a pub.

my short stay with this little airline, not long after I left to fly elsewhere an event occurred that was reminiscent of my Orca Air experiences: Baxter's 60 percent partners pulled the airline out from under him. Tom was given the ultimatum to turn the operations over to the investors, and, if he was a good boy, he could continue to fly for Thunderbird, but Linda was to exit by the fire door.

They picked the wrong man for such an ultimatum. Within five months the Baxters had their own licence, operating certificate and airplanes. They had immediately rented the office and booth space still available at the classy Nanaimo seaplane terminal and secured landing privileges at those hard-to-come-by docks in Vancouver's Coal Harbour area. By the time Thunderbird Air got around to doing whatever it had planned to do, Tom had scooped the business he had created back into his own hands, and the "T-Bird" name became history.

Hearing about all this from my perch in the sky while tracking between Vancouver airport and Qualicum Beach in an Islander, I gained some vicarious satisfaction that the two founders of this successful air service had won in the end, just like the Hardy Boys. And, like the Hardy Boys books, there was always an adventure in the next chapter, which was my encounter with Burrard Air, for whom I was now flying. The Britten Norman Islander was a ten-passenger, twin-engined machine built on the Isle of Wight but powered with American engines. Like the Beaver, it did precisely what the manufacturer said it would do, but it was not pretentious. It was typically British—very square, very tough, cold in cold weather, hot in hot weather, noisy as hell, safe, reliable and, for a pilot, completely lovable.

I was performing seven flights a day off the runways of Vancouver International to the little airport at Qualicum Beach in an attempt by Burrard Air to knock out the long-established and popular Aquila Air. The name Aquila may be familiar, because it was the airline for whom I had operated a seaplane out of Shawl Bay several years earlier. The ownership had changed hands twice since those days, and an enterprising businessman-pilot by the name of Harvey Gable had become the most recent owner. "Harv" was a most personable guy. He operated a scheduled service to Vancouver flying Cessna 401s, low-wing, six-passenger light twins. After a series of highly publicized court cases resulting from Transport Canada and Department of Labour investigations, Aquila closed down forever, but not before a couple of accidents in the last year of its operation.

I witnessed two of these accidents as I looked out the window of one of the hangars. The first happened on a hot summer day. A Cessna twin had commenced its takeoff run on the north-bound runway at Qualicum Beach while I and another pilot were talking in the Burrard Air office. The Cessna came roaring into my view at a position more than halfway along its takeoff run when, suddenly, the pilot cut the power and aborted the takeoff. He did not have enough runway left to stop the aircraft and ran off the end of the pavement, over a fifteen-foot embankment, and crashed into a stump-filled clearing, having barely made it over a road on which a car had just passed. I had known immediately, when the engines cut, that the craft would go off the runway, and I had darted out the door in time to see a big cloud of dust, followed by a very loud bang. The pilot and four passengers got out unscathed, and fortunately there was no fire. The plane was referred to as DBR—in flying lingo, "damaged beyond repair."

The second accident I witnessed was from the same vantage point, during a heavy, wet snowfall. The runway was awash with two inches of slush resulting from a very rapid change in the weather. Snowflakes the size of saucers had fallen for about twenty minutes,

144

and then rain had fallen, leaving a thick slush over the entire length of the asphalt runway. I had decided to delay my flight when I noticed a Cessna 172, belonging to Aquila, taxi out to the button of the southbound runway. This little four-place plane, with the pilot and one adult female passenger plus two small children aboard, commenced its takeoff run immediately. By the time the aircraft passed me it was developing full power, but the slush was being picked up and blown over the tail surface, making the plane look like a snow blower. The speed of the plane was well below what it would be doing on a dry runway, yet it continued to motor on down the runway until, a few feet from the end, the pilot yarded the craft off the ground.

The 172 staggered along, vainly attempting to climb over a stand of fir trees. It stalled and dove straight into the ground with a loud thump, then fell over onto its back. Smoke appeared. I ran to the phone and dialled Aquila, but as I was explaining what had taken place, a taxi driver who had been waiting between two of the hangars saw the crash and sped toward the smouldering wreck. He reached the accident scene and pulled the occupants out of the plane. Again Lady Luck was blowing on Aquila's dice—nobody was hurt, although two kids were crying their

eyes out and one frightened mother was trying to comfort them. Forty minutes later the sun was out, the runway was clear and airplanes were coming and going as usual.

During this last year of Aquila's life, Burrard Air began a competitive service into Qualicum Beach and hired me as its pilot. I had moved from Port McNeill down to Parksville by this time, and my location allowed the service to commence at seven o'clock each morning out of Qualicum, putting commuters in Vancouver by 7:35. The Islander was a better airplane than the Cessna 401s flown by the competition, though not so sexy to look at and considerably noisier. The seat rate established by Burrard was very competitive: twelve dollars less than Aquila's rate. Despite this, local residents were loyal to the rascal in the corner, and we had a hard time gaining acceptance. Burrard had an absentee-management problem, and repeated suggestions from me to get the rate back up to normal and alter the frequency didn't fall on deaf ears, it didn't fall on any ears at all. We plugged along at seven flights a day at what had been intended to be a special opening rate for the first week of service but which was never changed until the entire Burrard Air operation and all its B.C. routes folded.

Although this operation got me

The morning fog in Port Hardy sometimes kept the fleet on the ground until near noon.

home every night, the transition from flying in the "toolies" to operating out of Vancouver airport was a big hurdle. The heavy traffic out of YVR (the designator for Vancouver) kept me on my toes, and the total subservience to orders from the control tower was much different from what I had grown used to in the bush. Delays of as much as forty-five minutes were normal during the summer because larger airplanes in the circuit were all on instrument flight plans, which required seven-minute separation between take-offs. Also, when one of them called "Inbound," all the visual traffic had to wait until that airliner had its wheels on the ground. I got to know my passengers very well during these long, hot delays. One of them, a Friday afternoon "regular" who was a magazine publisher from Vancouver, would one day help to set me on another path.

Flying the Islander had its advantages. So quick was it off the ground that it became normal for the controllers to allow me an intersection departure, using only a short section of the runway, hanging a quick turnout and leaving a lineup of aircraft baking in the hot sun, waiting for a departure clearance. Some controllers were quick to extend this service to the Islander, but others hewed by the book until I and my passengers were done to a crisp and the Islander's idling engines were red hot.

A group of seven Parksville-Qualicum residents who did not want to see Burrard pull out of the Vancouver schedule approached me a few weeks before the closure. "We are prepared to buy this Islander from Burrard and set up our own service between Vancouver and Qualicum," they stated. "We don't have a licence or an operating certificate. Would Burrard Air let us operate under their licence until we got our own?" They were asking the wrong guy, but I agreed to carry their message. They wrote it all down as a proposal and gave it to me to present to Burrard Air's management. I gave the paper to the only management with whom I was in regular contact, the company dispatcher at Vancouver. He thought the proposal sounded pretty good. "Jump in your airplane and take it over to head office in Victoria," he said, which I immediately did.

The owners of Burrard read the proposal, then left the office together, asking me to wait. They weren't gone very long, and when they returned they looked angry. "We believe this is an insult to our intelligence," they stated, and I was made to understand that I was to get my ass out of their office. I was dumbfounded. Back in Qualicum Beach I spoke to Ken Fyfe, the spokesman for the group.

"Did they fire you?" he asked.

"No," I replied, "they just kicked me out of their office."

"Well," said Ken, "will you help us find an Islander? We'll just have to start from scratch." I gave him a few places to call, including the number of the factory on the Isle of Wight. About three weeks passed, during which I was still flying the Islander into Qualicum and doing some charter work with the machine into Ocean Falls. Then Ed Green stopped me in the office one day. He had a funny look on his face. "The boss says he fired you."

"He didn't fire me. He threw me out of his office."

"Oh," said Ed. "Well, he's fired you now, I guess."

"That's what the Romans used to do."

"What's that?" asked Ed, embarrassed by the situation.

"Shoot the messenger," I replied.

Another pilot performed the last flight into Qualicum Beach and dropped me off. That was the end of the Burrard Air, Qualicum sched. A few days later, that was the end of Burrard Air itself, as it shut down all the routes and put the fleet on the block. I spent the next week with Ken Fyfe, looking for an Islander to buy. We found one back in Cambridge, Maryland. Ken wired a $25,000 cheque as a deposit and bought the damned thing, sight unseen. He then hired me to go and get it.

147

14
OLD FRIENDS IN STRANGE PLACES

Young pilots are good at remembering model numbers. When you're full of fresh enthusiasm for airplanes, you can quote chapter and verse on types and models like a C47 or a T33 or an XP-109. You can also provide all the flight data and engine performance by rote when you're young and on top of it all.

As I stood in the Fedex warehouse at the Baltimore airport, I was hard pressed to remember my shoe size, much less the string of numbers identifying the slick little twin that came taxiing in to pick us up. It may have been a Cessna something or other, I'm not sure, but it exceeded by far anything I could ever expect to operate, so my mind automatically rejected the details. It sure was pretty, though, and all gussied-up inside for people who watch TV in flight and drink a lot to get over the sheer boredom of flying at 250 miles per hour over the Baltimore skyscrapers, the Annapolis naval training

college and the White House in Washington, and then out over Chesapeake Bay to Cambridge, Maryland.

All these names were not just written on the map; they were actually out there. I was swivelling my head from side to side, trying to get a look at the many famous places as we flew over the water at a thousand feet. It was here that the Kennedy clan had played; many well-known authors had lived here and chosen the area as the locale of their now-acclaimed books. The playground of the wealthy and politically influential in America was speeding below us, but the romance was somehow missing. Chesapeake Bay was a filthy-brown colour and looked pretty shallow. The only inspirational view was of the distant naval academy at Annapolis and the obelisk rising into the sky next to the White House.

As we let down over the bay and crossed the shoreline on final for a short, paved runway, an airplane parked

"Fly the Friendly Way with **TMA**"

TWIN-ENGINE 9 PASSENGER

Britten-Norman ISLANDER

among fifty others alongside that runway stood out like a sore thumb. It was white, with green engine nacelles, and the big vertical fin stood erect in typical Islander fashion—but that wasn't why I was grinning. The grin was for the big "A" on its tail, the oil pressure gauges installed right out on the engine nacelles, and the initials I knew would be painted on the tail and under the wing.

"That's DEB," I said, incredulously, to Ken Fyfe, who sat beside me. "Did you know you were buying DEB? What the hell is it doing all the way out here? I flew DEB at Port Hardy with Air BC. The oil pressure gauges were mounted on the outside of the engine by Bob Thompson; he couldn't stand those dickey little British panel instruments. DEB stands for Donald E. Braithwaite, who bought it in 1969. It doesn't have the big baggage compartment, y' know . . . Do you see that dent on the nose? That's where . . ." Ken Fyfe was looking at me strangely, thinking I'd gone nuts.

"That's . . . that's where a deer ran into it on takeoff." I craned around to catch a closer look as our wheels barked and we taxied past the parked airplane. I marvelled at the Trans-Mountain Airlines green paint, all the way from Campbell River, B.C., sitting here in Cambridge, Maryland, across Chesa-

Facing page: DEB over Vancouver, in an advertisement for Trans Mountain's Island schedule from Port Alberni and Qualicum to Vancouver, circa 1970. DEB was a 1969 airplane bearing Trans Mountain owner Donald E. Braithwaite's initials. This airplane would follow me around for most of my flying career. It showed up, unexpectedly, in Maryland, and I flew it across the United States, back to its original home in Campbell River.

peake Bay from the oval office—an unusual place to find an old friend.

It had been a whirlwind decision: Ken had closed the deal over the telephone and, having hung up, explained to me, "It's a 1969 BN2A Islander, that's all I know. I bought it, and it's in Cambridge. You and I will go and get it. Should be a great trip." I had known Ken for only a short time and was immediately impressed with how he got things done. He could not, however, indicate anything more about the plane he had just purchased.

"It's a little charter outfit who own it, they took it in on trade, haven't flown it themselves, don't know anything about it, just want to get rid of it, the price is right." So, what else would a guy want to know? "Oh yeah, he said, "they gave it a top overhaul and it runs like a charm."

Ken booked us both on United Airlines, out of Seattle to Boston, with the plan that we would rent a car for the trip to Cambridge. I read up on the area and got pretty excited about doing the tourist thing, retracing Paul Revere's freedom ride while reciting something from Ben Franklin's writings or maybe flying a kite in a thunderstorm. Alas, all that American history had to be put on hold when we attempted to rent a car in Boston.

"How far is it to the airport at

Cambridge?" Ken asked the Hertz attendant.

"There is no airport in Cambridge," she replied. "Boston airport is the airport for Cambridge. It's a suburb of Boston. Who are you looking for?" she asked, taking the paper from Ken's hand and squinting at the phone number written on it. "That's not a local number," she said, reaching for a phone book. She found what she was looking for and snapped the book shut.

"That area code is for Cambridge, all right," she said. "Cambridge Maryland, not Cambridge Massachusetts. You're in the wrong state of the union, mister."

We had to jump a commuter flight to Baltimore, where the aircraft owners would pick us up in their airplane. I was glad Paul Revere had known which Cambridge he was riding to, or this place might still be under the Union Jack.

That's how we got to Cambridge, Maryland, and how the airplane waiting for us turned out to be an old friend. It is also how we got to be sitting in the office of a Cambridge, Maryland, real estate company that also operated a charter airline and owned this terribly British airplane, which Ken had bought sight unseen.

"Funny story, how we came by that airplane," drawled our friendly pilot, who was also a partner in the business.

"I was out there in British Columbia,

Facing page: A Gulf
Air publicity photo
showing DEB in com-
pany with Otter QRI,
around 1970.

152

at an auction at a place called Ritchie
Brothers. Do you know it?" We
acknowledged that Ritchie Brothers, on
Twig Island, often held auctions in
which airplanes were sold.

"This here airplane you just bought
was up for auction at Ritchie's, and an
Englishman bought it. He was obviously English, from his accent, so I
asked him what he was going to do
with this here airplane. Damned if his
plans weren't to fly it across the
Atlantic Ocean to England." Our host
and storyteller continued with his
account of how he convinced the buyer
of the Islander to take him along on the
trip across the continent and back here
to Cambridge.

"I volunteered to be his co-pilot
and help him find his way across the
country, because—believe me—that
man was very inexperienced," he
explained. "By the time we got here,
I had convinced him that he needed a
little more airplane than that Islander to
cross the Atlantic. We gave him what
he had paid for it on trade for a proper
airplane, with the speed and range he
needed for such a trip," recalled our
host. "He did make it across the
Atlantic, by the way."

The next morning, I fuelled up DEB,
ran it up and performed a test flight. It
flew beautifully with only one problem:
the flap motor was unserviceable. Flap

motors for Britten Norman Islanders
were not to be found in Cambridge,
Maryland, or anywhere in the continental United States. Bridgemark
Aerospace, up in Toronto, was the
closest source of Islander parts, but it
too was fresh out of flap motors. It was
soon determined that the Wright
Brothers also flew without flaps, so I
would too.

When an aircraft is exported from
one country to another, it is an unwritten
law that the weight of the paperwork
must equal the gross weight of the aircraft before both governments agree to
release and/or accept the aircraft into or
out of their jurisdiction. Particular attention is given to the certificate of air-
worthiness of each country, there being a
requirement for an export "C of A" and an
import "C of A." Furthermore, the aircraft
is deregistered from the country of its
origin when it has arrived at its destination and re-registered in its new home.

DEB was the exception—it was an
illegal immigrant. It had arrived from
Canada into the United States having
been deregistered in Canada by Air BC
prior to being sold at the Ritchie Brothers auction. The Englishman had just
got in it and flew across the country; he
wasn't intending to sell it. No one had
seen fit to register it in the United
States, so it was an orphan.

"If you young fellers tell all this to

OLD FRIENDS IN STRANGE PLACES

154

Many years later (1995), the Islander showed up in the hangar where I was publishing *West Coast Aviator* magazine. It was then owned by Airlink, an air courier operator.

the Federal Aviation Administration here in Washington, D.C., you'd stand a better chance of gaining a hearing with the president than ever getting that thing offa the ground," said our good American friend.

"They'll have so much red tape wound around you and that airplane you'll look like that Egyptian King Tut, before he came unwound." We considered this fact and deemed our friend to be wise beyond his years. When we

called the FAA to request a flight permit to fly the plane across the United States to Blaine, Washington, they didn't even ask about the registration. They merely assumed it was a Canadian civil-registered aircraft, C-FDEB. They asked us for a flight itinerary and issued a highly detailed flight permit, itemizing every stop along the way. We were permitted to make these stops, and these only, on our odyssey across America. The fax they sent us on the day of departure was eight feet long, listing some eighteen stops across the country.

Our journey across the United States from east to west became somewhat circuitous because terrible storms were raging across the land. We left Cambridge on February 28, 1989, crossing Chesapeake Bay, and then went directly over the White House at six thousand feet, with airliners punching up beside us like arrows out of Washington International Airport—the scariest part of the trip. Overflying the Adirondacks, we recalled the exciting and often tragic history of the early mail flights through these mountains. By comparison with the B.C. Coast Range these were rolling hills, but it was here that Charles Lindbergh, mail pilot, had bailed out into the stormy night sky.

We tracked across West Virginia, then Kentucky, Kansas and Colorado, taking several long diversions as far south as Laredo, Texas, before reaching Salt Lake City. The peaks between Colorado and Salt Lake City had claimed the lives of many Mormon pioneers, whose covered-wagon trails are still visible alongside the railroad right-of-way. Less than two hundred feet separated us from those icy peaks when Salt Lake City suddenly appeared, 12,000 feet below. Resisting the temptation to descend rapidly, and out of respect for those hard-working cylinders, we flew across the salt flats, over the longest runway I have ever seen, which was that of the air force base at McChord Field. Then, descending all the time, we received our clearance and landed at the civil airport. Ken suggested that we get something to eat and find a bed before seeking out the Mormon Tabernacle Choir. I bought into the food idea and the room, but passed on the choir. It had been a long trip, and we still had the states of Oregon and Washington before us in the morning.

When we finally got back to Qualicum Beach, Ken decided, after a lot of deliberations, against starting an airline service to Vancouver. Instead, he leased out the Islander to get some return on his investment, and I started thinking seriously about retiring from this crazy business.

At the time, I believed that Ken had made a mistake in not establishing a scheduled service between Vancouver and Qualicum Beach. I still think that, but at the time there were many hoops to jump through and Ken chose not to perform those tricks. In the meantime, a Qualicum Beach resident who operated a fishing resort in the Northwest Territories was looking for a Beaver pilot. I applied for the job. What the hell, I thought, if I get it, fine; if not, I'll do something else. This declaration had a familiar ring.

155

15

VARIATION EAST BRAIN IS LEAST

I was a very high-time seaplane pilot when I took the job at Kasba Lake in the Northwest Territories. The truth was, I wasn't going to log much more time because I figured this was the last flying job I would hold. I would retire soon and go into the publishing business. The reference to "high time" is just to establish that I decided I had very few tricks to learn, and this would be a cakewalk. This is not a good attitude in the flying business. Not for the first time, I would have my balloon burst by unforeseen events and by my own overconfidence. My biggest lessons in flying would be learned right at the end of my career.

We arrived at La Ronge, Saskatchewan, to pick up CF-MAS and fly it four hundred miles north to Kasba Lake. MAS was a de Havilland DHC2 Beaver, built in 1948 for Manitoba Air Services (thus, MAS) and had recently been rebuilt with all the Kenmore modifications on it. This work had been done by the famous Al Beaulieu, of Vancouver. These modifications were chiefly cosmetic; the Beaver was a superior bush plane from the day it came out of the factory. However, a significant operational change had been made by installing a three-bladed propeller and relocating the battery from aft of the rear seats up to the firewall. To do this, a smaller battery was used and the generator system was discarded in favour of an alternator, which resulted in a significant saving in weight and a much-improved baggage compartment. The "Kenmore mods," conceived by the Seattle floatplane operator of that name, continue to be a very popular modification to the Beaver.

On this day, the owner of Kasba Lake Lodge, Doug Hill, and four pretty young women were aboard the plane, which was also carrying a few supplies. It was May 12 and spring was in the air at La Ronge, but I was warned that

Facing page: Doug
Hill's Beaver, MAS,
originally from Man-
itoba Air Services,
was the first Beaver
Al Beaulieu had
rebuilt with all the
Kenmore modifica-
tions. The major
changes included the
replacement of the
old generator with
an alternator system,
a smaller battery
relocated onto the
firewall, a three-
bladed prop, a split-
bench seat and
bubble windows.
Both magnetos self-
destructed simultane-
ously one day, during
a flight to Obre Lake
with five passengers
aboard.

158

Kasba Lake would probably still be frozen solid, being located north of latitude sixty degrees. There were no maps aboard the plane, but Doug assured me that he knew the way and that there were charts available up at the lodge. "Just fly due north," he stated, waving his hand in a northerly direction. I set up the heading on 360 degrees and we augured along until there, in front of us, was a dirt strip and a little lake, a watering hole called Points North, where we refuelled for the final leg to Kasba. When we arrived at Kasba Lake, the rumour proved to be true: the lake was solid ice, fifteen inches thick.

"Just fly over there," said Doug, pointing toward a shoreline where a couple of islands protruded from the ice. As we got closer, I could see patches of water where the ice had broken up and drifted away. "You can land in there," he said, pointing out the longest stretch of clear water. "It may be a bit shallow, but it's just a grass bottom." I throttled back and pumped on some flap, descending to within a couple of feet of the surface and dragged the area, carefully examining the water. There was a yellow tinge to the surface, which I guessed was the grassy bottom, but it looked deep enough for the Beaver, so I hauled her around and landed, ever so gently.

She landed and came off the step

nicely—no problems. As we taxied for the shore, where Doug had pointed out a trail that led to the lodge, we suddenly bottomed and came to a stop, high and dry in the middle of this frozen lagoon. I turned around and looked at Doug and the four young women with deep regret. There was only one thing to do—lighten the load—and they were the load.

They climbed out with great reluctance and stepped into the near-freezing arctic water. Being only up to their ankles in water, Doug and the girls began the walk to shore. As they proceeded, however, the water got deeper, and deeper, until they were chest deep. I stayed close to them, taxiing along, warm and happy in my airplane, which had floated off the bar as soon as the passengers had stepped out. The water shallowed again, and the frozen waders were now only waist-deep. They were now shivering and catcalling to me as the rat of the century, as I taxied to shore and shut down the engine. The ladies plunged into the thicket on the shoreline and made off down the icy trail at high speed, their clothing freezing to their bodies as they ran.

We opened the cookhouse and dining room and eventually got the fires going, and the women disappeared to change into dry clothing. They were good sports about the icy dip, but it must have been a rude awakening. All of these women had worked here in previous years and knew their way around the place. Before the night was upon us they had made the lodge cozy, and Linda, the cook, had fed us all. Doug went up to the esker above the camp and unearthed a drum of avgas to refuel MAS.

The avgas had been buried in the ground the previous year to prevent theft by marauding Chipewyans who regularly plundered the few lodges in the area during the winter, in search of gas for their snowmobiles, food for themselves and anything else of value they could find lying about. Great precautions had been taken at Kasba to hide boats and outboard motors, and although there was evidence of a break-in, nothing had been found worth stealing. Doug Hill had made certain of

that at the end of the previous season. As we loaded the forty-five-gallon drum onto the dolly behind the three-wheeled ATV, Doug pointed out hundreds of dark spots on the distant ice of the lake.

"Those are caribou," he said. "They've been shot for target practice. No meat has been taken from them. They haven't been touched. Just shot for the hell of it. Last year, there were twenty thousand caribou shot that way—for no reason at all." I could see he was getting angry as he related this story. "The Canadian government doesn't want to talk about it, for fear

they'll hurt somebody's feelings." He stomped off in disgust about the situation as I peered across the ice. As far as I could see, there were dark spots on the ice. The ice around these animals would absorb the warm sunlight faster than the surrounding ice and melt first during the breakup, which was due to start any time now.

When morning arrived, Doug passed me a handful of maps and told me to hightail back to Points North to pick up a full load of groceries. The charts were not aviation maps but forestry charts, which, while very detailed, were on an extremely small scale. From up in

The Beaver was available for charter by prospectors, survey teams and other sports fishing lodges. When not otherwise engaged, I would fly fuel for a helicopter working fifty miles up the lake or track two hundred miles to find empty fuel drums left by survey teams in previous years. I never worked harder than on this airplane at Kasba. If things got really slow, there was always the airport to roll with a truck and compactor. The blackflies finally got to me, and I went down for three days with something strange. Whatever it was, it didn't quit for six years.

the air, the country looks like a jigsaw puzzle with half the pieces missing, these being filled with water or ice, depending on the time of year. Frozen as it was and with snow still covering the ground, the land was totally featureless and not a bit like the coastal areas I knew so well. The plane had an ADF and there were a few beacons around, including one at Kasba, which I determined would have to be my method of navigation, coupled with flying a compass heading. What an error in judgment this proved to be.

Two things went haywire: the compass was unreliable, due to fluctuating variation in these northern regions, and the ADF needle just turned through 360 degrees and would not lock on to anything. The featureless country ultimately defied my map reading, and I knew I was in trouble. When I had exceeded my time en route and fuel was getting low, I figured discretion to be the better part of valour and looked for a lake on which to land. I listened out on several VHF frequencies and heard somebody talking to another plane. I interrupted and got their attention, describing my plight. The pilot I contacted tried to identify the lake I was landing on from my description, but to no avail. His signal was very strong and he figured he was close and could find me, but he too was low on fuel. He said

he would come back in an hour and search for me and that I should listen out in an hour. He would bring some gas with him and lead me to his base on Wollaston Lake.

That was the longest hour of my life; darkness was not far off, and I sure as hell didn't want to spend the night snubbed onto this strange and unfriendly shore. I ate a can of pears from the emergency rations and tried to remain cool.

As an afterthought, the pilot had suggested I turn on my emergency locater transmitter and leave it on until he got back. He told me later that a Russian satellite had picked up my signal and provided Canadian search-and-rescue officials with what turned out to be an inaccurate set of coordinates, which led my saviour back to a spot some twenty miles away. He was a pretty resourceful guy and flew a build-and-fade course to determine approximately where I was.

"There you are, down there on Johnson Lake," he said, as his plane roared into view. I breathed a sigh of relief, then immediately felt like an idiot for doing the unforgivable— getting lost. Me, the zillion-hour Beaver pilot! As the rescuing Cessna flared for the landing and taxied toward the beach, it crossed my mind that at least nobody on the coast would hear about

161

162

this, and I sure as hell wasn't going to tell them. With that consoling thought, I got out of the plane and splashed through the muskeg and brambles toward the other aircraft.

A young lad came crashing along the shoreline from the other direction, carrying two red jerry cans of avgas. As he handed them to me and we looked at each other, we both burst out laughing. He was from Sechelt, and we had met several times on the seaplane dock at Nanaimo. My secret was out: the damned small world that is aviation had tripped me up, and I would never live this one down.

"I've just arrived up here too, but this outfit I'm with is making me ride shotgun with a local pilot before letting me get lost on my own," the young pilot explained. "My pilot knows this country like the back of his hand." It was a kind thing for him to say, because it allowed me to justify my stupidity. After all, I had not been given a chance to learn the area, nor had I been given decent maps, and that damned ADF was unserviceable—and what about that compass variation? I knew I was beating my gums to no avail and continued to feel like an idiot.

Darkness descends like a curtain in

A classic Norseman aircraft, predecessor to the Beaver, arrived at Kasba Lake to pick up two passengers. This beautifully restored Norseman turned out to be CF-SAP, a former West Coast airplane with much history, from the Tofino area. This photograph gives some idea of the problems relating to operating on glassy water. LINDA THE KASBA COOK PHOTO

the north. By the time I got the gas into the Beaver, it was dark.

"Follow me back to the base," yelled the pilot of the Cessna 206. "I'll probably get way ahead of you, but when you get to a big lake you'll see two little islands and some lights. That's where you're going." With that he bombed out of the lake, his strobe lights winking in the blackness. I put the boots to the Beaver and followed him out with my eyes glued to those winking lights. There was no way I was going to lose this guy. If I could get lost in broad daylight in this godforsaken place, what chance would I have at night? I carried "Meto" (maximum engine takeoff) power and called him on the VHF to slack off a bit. He never knew how close to him I was; when he got to that "big lake and the two little islands," I was right behind him in the turn and his ruts on the water didn't get a chance to fill in because I was in them. It was blacker than Toby's when I finally docked at the seaplane base, and they gave me a mat on the floor of the boss's house on which to nurse my damaged ego.

The next morning, I bought a map from the little airline, thanked my rescuer and took off for Points North, flying with one finger on the chart and my eyes glued to the terrain ahead. Thinking about my escapade, I checked

the chart and determined that I had been about forty miles off course to the east, over a distance of three hundred miles—not bad for a beginner. I never relied on my compass again for the next three months and flew without the use of the ADF until the very last day on the job, and therein hangs the denouement of this little adventure.

On that last day at Kasba Lake, three months later, I was inbound from a survey camp with my last load of gear and the survey crew, before heading home forever. It was a beautiful, clear and sunlit day, and I was now familiar enough with this terrain to daydream a bit as the Beaver skimmed along, a couple of hundred feet above the muskeg. I reached forward to the panel and absentmindedly flipped the rocker switch marked "Alternator" to the "off" position. The ADF stopped going around in circles and pointed hard at the Kasba NDB (non-directional beacon) fifty miles ahead. That damned alternator was the culprit. It was, somehow, creating its own magnetic field and making the ADF seek itself. The ADF had been trying, all this time, to fly up its own ass. In this case, it had flown up mine.

163

16

ARCTIC ADVENTURES AND
ANCESTRAL REVISITATIONS

My grandfather would have thoroughly approved of my last flying job. Anything with the word "survey" in it would bring his gnarled old hands up to grip an imaginary theodolite and he would clear his throat, place his pipe somewhere where the spittle would leave a brown stain and launch into an account of surveying the CPR right-of-way. Back when he was operating a portable sawmill, cutting ties "just ahead of steel" for the new trans-Canada railway, my mother's father had been a self-made man. He had taught himself any science he needed to perform his task and had innovated his way into wealth and out of it on several occasions during his lifetime.

Something he had learned from his life's adventures was to go not west, young man, but north. He had encouraged me for years to "go north—that's where the future is in this country." I had disappointed him by remaining relatively south in my endeavours. Had

he been living, he would have approved of Whitehorse, Dawson City and Inuvik, where all but one of my final flying adventures lay waiting.

"We need somebody who can just fly a straight line back and forth," said the voice over the phone. "You will be flying an Aero Commander—a nice little twin, with a GNS system installed. The plane used to belong to the president of Ecuador," he added, which I took to mean that it was a cream puff. The phone call was from the chief pilot of an aerial survey company, whom I had met while flying out of Kasba Lake during my tenure of duty in that fish camp.

"The plane is located up in Whitehorse," he said. "The pilot won't be around to check you out when you get there." I didn't know what GNS stood for at that time; global navigational systems were at the cutting edge of technology then and definitely not installed in the kind of airplanes I had been flying. I replied, "Oh, that would

FLIGHTS OF A COAST DOG

be just great," thinking that I could find out how it worked before heading north. Also, since I had never flown any of the Aero Commander models of light twins and my would-be employer couldn't remember what model the plane was, I figured I would need a PPC (pilot proficiency check) on type before going to Whitehorse. The plane could turn out to be either a turbo-charged or turbine-powered model, both of which were completely out of my experience.

"Okay, you can get a checkout in Edmonton, on your way up to Whitehorse," he said, and we clinched the deal. I was to spend a couple of days flying with an aerial photography outfit in Edmonton that operated the same type of airplane. The date was September 29, 1989. I arrived at Edmonton's municipal airport, conveniently located near the city's downtown, right next door to my hotel. A young pilot checked me out in an Aero Commander 800F. We performed an hour of "touch and goes" and "circuits and bumps" up at Edmonton's near-new and near-deserted international airport. The airplane was the closest I would ever get to a corporate luxury airplane, and although I was ham-fisted with the craft in the beginning, I never hammered it on. By the second hour of flying on the following day, I was thinking how nice it would be to fly something like this

and wear a clean white shirt for a change.

The next morning, I boarded a Canadian Airlines F27 for the trip to Fort St. John, where I would change planes for Whitehorse. It was on this flight that I sat behind someone I deemed to be the "deceased" Ed Carder, whose story is told in an earlier chapter. Arriving in Whitehorse in the late afternoon, I checked into a hotel close to the airport and walked over to the field to locate my airplane. An employee of the local FBO (fixed base operator) drove me over to the hangar where I had been told it would be located, and lo and behold, as he dropped me off, what did I spy but my old friend, the Islander DEB, sitting there in its multi-coloured, peeling paint job, just as we had found it in Cambridge, Maryland, a few months back. Keeping it company on the tarmac was an Aero Commander 500 "Shrike," with a twelve-foot stinger protruding obscenely from its tail. This had to be my airplane. On the tail was the confirmation, the identifier C-GSJK.

I slid into the seat that had once belonged to the president of Ecuador and felt right at home, despite not speaking a word of Spanish. The airplane was powered by two Lycoming IO-540s, which were old friends because this was the power plant used in the Cessna 185. Since I knew all the

Previous page: I was
sent to Edmonton to
get checked out on
this airplane, an Aero
Commander 800F, in
preparation for flying
a similar type that
was waiting for me at
Whitehorse.

168

numbers needed to operate these
engines, that fancy checkout in Edmonton had not been totally necessary. I
found the pilot's manual in the glove
box and took it with me to study back
at the hotel. Before leaving the tarmac,
I strolled over to the Islander and
looked inside, wondering as I did so
why this airplane kept following me
around. I learned much later that Ken
Fyfe had leased it to an operator up
here who had a freight contract. DEB
had been badly treated, according to its
owner, and certainly its appearance,
squatting here at Whitehorse beside the
pretty Shrike, attested to that fact.

The next morning I met Charlotte,
the geophysicist who would accompany
me on the survey flights out of Dawson
City and Inuvik. She explained that the
body of the survey had been performed
over the past six months, but a few
areas were left to do to complete the
government contract. She knew the
aircraft systems well, having flown in
the Shrike for many months, and
elected to check me out in the plane.

"This is Dan McGrew country," I said
to her, gesturing down to the lakes
beneath us as we climbed out of
Whitehorse, bound for Dawson City.
We were following the highway from
Whitehorse up to Dawson, and well-
known places like Carcross and Mayo
passed beneath our wings. Though

totally new to me, the country seemed
friendly. Had I believed in reincarnation
I would figure I had been here before,
probably as one of those poor sods in
that popular photo, struggling up a
nearly vertical mountain in search of
gold and, in case you have doubts, not
finding any.

Charlotte operated the magnetometer and camera and recording
equipment in the back of the plane
during the survey flights. Over the next
few weeks I would learn that her father
was a pilot, as was her brother, who had
been recently killed in a plane crash.
Charlotte was herself a private pilot,
licensed to fly helicopters. She had
been very happy with the former pilot
of this plane and was as nervous as a cat
with me flying it. She watched me like
a hawk and doubted decisions I made
on some of the mechanical breakdowns
we had later. I put a lot of it down to
the stress resulting from the recent
death of her brother, but I never felt
comfortable flying the Shrike until later,
when I flew it by myself across Canada.

This job was going to last a month,
from October 3 to November 3, and
would involve tracking thirty-mile-long
parallel legs at a specified altitude on
headings steered with the aid of the GNS.
The magnetometer in the "stinger" on the
tail and the belly camera would record
their findings under Charlotte's control

and would ultimately be sent to Ottawa.

The weather had been clear and cold, about thirteen below zero, on average, with brilliant sunlight and cloudless skies. On October 13, after completing the work out of Dawson, we planned to track the Dempster Highway up to Inuvik for the last few days of the project. We ran into bad weather at the Richardson Range, where freezing rain lowered visibility through the mountains. Turning around and arriving back at Dawson, we found ourselves on top of a heavy overcast that totally obscured Dawson City and the airport. I headed through some now-familiar mountain passes to the south of Dawson, thinking I would go for Mayo, but I soon spotted a hole through the cloud cover into the valley that led to the airport at Dawson. We sneaked through the mountain passes, letting down as rapidly as the terrain would allow, and snuck into the valley below the cloud. We had about six hundred feet above ground level for the short trip to the airport and landed at Dawson without incident.

This airplane had an auxiliary saddle tank that gave us a six-hour range at two hundred miles per hour, allowing several options for alternative airports, but visual flight overtop of cloud in this country is not the best plan to fly by and was, in those days, illegal. One of this survey company's airplanes, a Trilander, had been caught in this manner and had landed on the "Top of the World Highway" near Dawson City, carrying off a perfect landing, except for clipping a road sign warning road users to watch for falling rock. The plane was sufficiently damaged to be disassembled on the road and trucked off the mountain for repairs.

Because of the low temperatures, we had to wrap the airplane in tarpaulins at the end of each flying day and pull on engine covers, dome-fastening them into place. Also, 1500-watt electric heaters were installed in each engine nacelle, in the cockpit and in the back of the cabin with the fancy recording equipment. All of this electrical load was handled by plugging into the AC outlets in the aircraft parking area. The job of wrapping and unwrapping the plane was time consuming. It required folding and stowing all the tarps and rolling up miles of extension cables with the heaters and then performing the reverse procedure at the end of the day. The tarpaulins saved the wings from frosting up during the cold nights and, in case of snowfall, reduced the job of digging out.

On the next day, October 14, we made it into Inuvik and wrapped the critter for the night, taking a taxi into town and checking into the Alexander

Facing page: The
Shrike and the com-
pany truck at
Dawson City. Char-
lotte drove the truck
up from Whitehorse,
and I flew the air-
craft. The weather
was balmy when we
first arrived.

170

Mackenzie Hotel at one hundred
dollars per night, twice the downtown
Edmonton price in this year of 1989. It
snowed during the night, and we found
our airplane to be something of an ice
sculpture in the morning.

The window of opportunity for using
the GNS equipment was based on the
availability of the seven satellites on
which the equipment triangulated. This
resulted in all of the survey work being
done between nine o'clock in the
morning and one in the afternoon out
of Inuvik and required us to fly for
three days to complete the job. Everything went swimmingly until the day
we were leaving.

Pilots prefer to do their own
refuelling. If you have filled the tanks
yourself, you know they are full, you
know that no water or snow has been
brushed in from atop the wing and that
the cap is on properly when you are finished. The Shrike was designed by a
famous aircraft designer, Ted Smith,
whose aircraft are superb, but he went
home for lunch when the fuel filler cap
was designed for this airplane. The
cap, when properly positioned, is
locked in place by setting a Phillips
head screw, but it is quite possible for
the cap to appear to be in position
when in fact it is not locked down. I
had been very careful with checking
and rechecking the fit whenever we

refuelled, but on this morning the gas
dealer insisted that he would fill it while
Charlotte and I loaded the plane. When
he finished, he took his stepladder and
left. Our own little stepladder was now
buried beneath tarpaulins, cables and
personal baggage in the cargo compartment, so my walk-around did not
include checking the fuel filler cap.

Ten minutes after takeoff I was to
pay for my oversight. Scanning the
panel, I was shocked to see that we
were now down to half tanks—we were
obviously venting fuel. I cranked the
Shrike around and headed back to
Inuvik. Charlotte, craning around in her
seat, verified that a silver streak of raw
fuel was spewing out of the wing. We
landed back at Inuvik without incident
but with the nagging realization that a
fuel filler cap for an Aero Commander
Shrike would be one scarce item and
we might spend a long time up here,
frozen in at the top of the world, before
one could be located and sent to us.

I set about walking the taxiways in
the off-chance it had fallen off as we
taxied out for takeoff, but that kind of
luck wasn't around this day. I did get an
idea, however, and trekked over to the
airport maintenance base to ask for
their help in searching the field. The
head honcho was not optimistic, and I
wasn't getting very far with him.

"You really don't know where it fell

ARCTIC ADVENTURES AND ANCESTRAL REVISITATIONS

off. It could be ten miles off the end of the runway. I don't think we can help you," he told me. Meanwhile, one of the snowblower drivers who had been standing there, listening, a young woman dressed for the thirty-below day, got up and left the office. She was back in less than ten minutes, as I was about to trudge out of the office.

"Is this what you're looking for?" she asked, handing me the most magnificent fuel filler cap I'd ever seen. "It was sitting there at the side of the runway, just about where you would have taken off." She had cold, rosy cheeks and I wanted to kiss both of them. I went back to the fuel distributor, where Charlotte had waited. The dealer, very upset at the part he had played, refilled our tanks free of charge. I put the cap on myself this time, while Charlotte called head office in Brantford, Ontario, on her cellular. She had apparently already called them to advise of the disaster and was now undoing the dismay they must have been suffering at this turn of events.

My log book shows a 2.2-hour flight from Inuvik to Dawson City that day, and I recall the brilliant sunshine turning to a dull grey as we swathed the Shrike in wing covers and tarpaulins and plugged her in for the night before heading for the Eldorado Hotel in the company van.

173

Previous page: Inuvik was recording twenty-seven degrees below zero, with heavy snowfalls in the evenings. This gassing-up was about to create a major problem. The cap blew off on takeoff, and our fuel vented overboard.

A message was waiting for Charlotte at the hotel. She was to drive the van down to Whitehorse and jump on the first available airline flight back to Toronto, while I was to fly the Shrike back to Brantford, Ontario. The next morning dawned with a fresh fall of snow, the cloud base at rooftop and visibility down to zilch. There was no flying in this stuff, but Charlotte bid adieu and took off in the truck for Whitehorse and her home in the lake district north of Toronto.

I kicked around Dawson City for the rest of the day, checking out Pierre Berton's family home and even trekking up to the graveyard overlooking the city. I rubbed the fresh-fallen snow off a couple of the tombstones of the famous "lost patrol," realizing from the dates inscribed just how young these Mounties had been when they lost their lives in this frozen land. It was getting decidedly colder as the day wore on, so I made my way back to the Eldorado Hotel, taking up a viewing position on the bed in front of the TV. Robert Service would have composed a verse for this, I recall thinking as I nodded off to sleep.

"What the hell was that?" I had awakened with a start. The TV was displaying horizontal hash marks, but I couldn't hear the static of the audio for the din in the hall. Very loud laughter came from many people. Somebody yelled, "Do it again, Eddie!" This was followed by a heavy thump. My light fixture rocked as the crowd roared its approval at whatever Eddie had done again. I opened the door, peering out into the empty hallway. A room down the hall had its door ajar, and some of the din was coming from there, while there was obviously more cacophony coming from the floor above. Returning to my room, I turned off the TV, took off my crumpled clothes and went back to bed. The football game upstairs continued, and Eddie did it again and again and again and . . .

Two feet of dry snow sat on the roofs of the buildings below my third-storey window and a blur of snowflakes filled the view from my window. Nuts, I thought, feeling the old pressure of that need to perform at all costs. Somebody else, Joe or Ed, they'd fly on a day like this. What was I, some kind of a candy ass? Such were my thoughts as I dialled up Brantford and told them the bad news. I hung up and went down for breakfast. As I passed the desk, the woman on duty called me over and handed me an envelope with my room number scrawled across it. The envelope was from some mining company, according to the logo in the corner. The message inside was amazing.

"Sorry for the racket last night we

know you didn't get a decent sleep we have paid for your room for the night thanks." It was signed by someone unknown. I went back to the desk, noticing that a similar envelope stuck out of the mail boxes of every occupied room on the third floor. "It's a mining company who are out in the bush all year. When they shut down for the season, they really shut down," she explained with a grin. "They do this every year."

This second day of waiting was spent visiting those few stores and tourist traps still open at this time of the year. "Everybody heads south to Nevada or Arizona now," was the explanation for the near ghost-town feel to Dawson City as I trudged around, taking a few photos of the historic places. I was getting pretty antsy to get moving. My judgment of the next day's weather gave it more hope than it deserved. I grabbed my gear and checked out with the proviso that my room be kept available for a couple of hours, in case I returned. The taxi dropped me off at the airport, beside a snow structure in the vague shape of an airplane. The digging out and disrobing of the plane, the storage of all the tarps and cables and the warmup took the best part of an hour. I was damp and sweating as the Shrike sped down the runway and climbed into a leaden sky.

While I had read optimism into the weather reports, a bare fifteen minutes down the valley I ran into lowering ceilings and a heavy snowstorm. Reluctantly I turned back for Dawson, not having found a vestige of the predicted higher overcast. The FSS station at Dawson confirmed my decision, for Whitehorse was now reporting "zero-zero" in snow. I reluctantly wrapped up my airplane and returned to the now-obviously mediocre cuisine of the Eldorado dining room.

On October 27, four days after Charlotte had taken off in the van, the hotel manager drove me up to the airport and I took off on the first leg of the trip to Toronto. The fuel-injected engines were singing in the cold air, and occasionally sunlight would break through to glint off the fresh snow on the hills below.

The mountains in the Yukon are not like the Coast Range; they are conelike in shape and rise directly from the terrain, without foothills, to as high as seven thousand feet. A few weeks before we had flown over these peaks and followed the Dempster Highway north to Inuvik. Now, as I climbed southeast through the valley toward Mayo, the Dempster could be glimpsed behind me, performing its northbound convolutions through those magnificent rocky cones. Ahead, the terrain was

176

partially obscured with low cloud and snowstorms.

During my idle days in Dawson, I had checked over the Shrike's panel and had been able to get one of its radio direction finders to operate. All other navigational equipment had been disconnected when the GPS was installed, and the GPS would read only on north-south headings. Now, I tuned this one operational navaid onto the Mayo beacon, and the needle swung hard to port and locked onto the signal. I was abeam the Mayo beacon, about ten miles west. My finger found the Shrike's position on the knee chart, and I was immediately struck with the incongruity of the situation. Here I was, with a state-of-the-art navigational panel capable of navigating from satellites in space, but forced to fly visually across Canada in the worst months of winter. Despite this, as I looked out over the sleek, sloping, Toronto-seeking nose of the Shrike, I relished the thought of all Canada yet before me.

In the West, until you reach Thunder Bay, there are numerous radio beacons called NDBs (non-directional beacons). The signals from these beacons are quite low in power because their primary use is for aircraft performing instrument approaches to the airports with which they are associated. The CBC, however, has powerful transmitters

right across Canada, and the ADF in this airplane could be tuned to their AM frequencies and track right across the land while I was listening to the broadcast. On this first morning, as I passed Mayo, I punched up the CBC frequency, and a blurt of familiar music came through my headphones. It was the *Morningside* theme, blowing me out of the cockpit and swinging my ADF needle to a heading to steer to make good for Whitehorse. I named this backup navigational system "Omnidirectional Gzowski," for it was Peter Gzowski's dulcet tones that accompanied me on this and several subsequent morning flights.

When I got to Whitehorse, the airport was partially obscured. In fact, half of the field was zero-zero in fog, while the other half was as clear as a bell. The runway was obscured but the taxiway, which had once been a runway, was wide open. I landed on the taxiway with a grudging approval from the tower, picked up some gear belonging to the survey company and then took off again for Fort Nelson.

Down the Liard River valley, over the country made famous during the search for famed aviator Paddy Burke in 1930, I pointed my little airplane, feasting on the historic terrain unrolling beneath the Shrike's sleek belly. On to Fort Nelson, Fort St. John and the Peace

ARCTIC ADVENTURES AND ANCESTRAL REVISITATIONS

River country, names I was weaned on by stories of early flyers and a travelling salesman father who had done it all before me, in 1915, with a horse and buckboard, and later a Model T.

Out of Edmonton's municipal airport, climbing over the unfamiliar city of my birth, I did not recognize the Royal Alexandra Hospital from the memory of such a brief stay in its nursery more than sixty years ago. Down there, somewhere in those ingeniously numbered streets, was a place referred to by my mother as "back on 118th Avenue," from where my plus-fours-clad brothers still peer out from sepia-toned snapshots in the family album.

The strength of the CBC signal, coupled with the unerring accuracy of the CPR rail line, provide an old Beaver pilot with all he needs for navigation. A combination of Gzowski, Vicki Gabereau and William Van Horne was now leading me across a land in which my ancestors made their histories. I planned a first fuel stop for Yorkton, Saskatchewan—a stop not truly necessary, as the saddle tank was still to the brim, but Yorkton is the home of my wife's family and I wanted to say I rolled the wheels on their home turf.

As dusk approached, Michael Enright's electronic finger pointed out my course across Canada. I thought how much fun it would be to call in to his program, *As It Happens*, and ask him if he knew the route taken by those early North West Mounted Police in their trek westward back in the "pre-Shrike" days of 1874. I sought out, from a height of three thousand feet, the footprints of my paternal grandfather, who had been with those early "red-coats." He helped drive out the Yankee whisky traders from Fort Whoop-Up and welcomed the Sioux nation into Alberta as refuge from Custer and the U.S. 7th Cavalry before establishing himself at Pincher Creek, Alberta. He then went on to create a chain of four general stores, a large bank account and a fierce, unforgiving Presbyterian attitude toward his grandchildren.

My mother's father had left a more indelible mark on the frozen land that sped beneath my warm cockpit. He had cut ties from a portable mill just ahead of steel as the CPR moved west. It is unlikely that any of his original handiwork was among those I now followed, marching across the land, but I homed on their replacements as far as the Lakehead: Fort William in his day, Thunder Bay in mine.

There was too much cloud below me to allow a glimpse of Kenora, my mother's childhood home. I remembered her calling it Rat Portage and how, as kids, we shrank from such a name, much preferring the contrived one of Kenora. I was occasionally granted a glimpse of Lake of the Woods, where my grandmother had painted, skilfully in oils and water-colours, the early beauty of the place, in 1850—pictures that tempted me in my youth to emulate her artistry and that hang yet upon my home walls. I wondered how she would have depicted my "Shrike's-eye view" of her favourite place.

Total cloud cover below forced me into an illegal "visual flight over cloud," as a caller from Buffalo talked to Enright and, unknowingly, guided me on across my native land. The auto-pilot took over as I gingerly unscrewed the cap of my thermos, which had been capped at near sea level that morning, and sipped a unique cup of Fort Nelson coffee, savoured at thousands of feet over Dryden, Ontario—an evil Ontario, I remembered:

"The bloody freight rates are half the cost westbound from Ontario as they are eastbound. Everything this bloody government does is for Ontario or Quebec." This is my father ranting to his father-in-law, my grandfather. I am down on the floor, reading the weekend comics and taking it all in, though appearing to be entranced with Terry and the Pirates. My mother is in the kitchen, cooking the weekend roast.

"It has to be that way," replies my grandfather, blowing smoke and tobacco out of his pipe as he replies. He clenches on the pipe as he speaks and it bounces up and down, unloading the smoking embers onto his vest and the glossy *Northern Miner* tabloid on his lap. "King has that figured right," he says, and is about to explain why Mackenzie King has it right, but the mere mention of Mackenzie King sends my father into paroxysms of anger.

"We've had enough of Mackenzie King," he storms. "He's looking after Ontario and playing vote-catching games with Quebec, at our expense. It's time the West had something to say. Bloody Ontario," he says, as he gets up and vents his anger by shaking the Hudson's Bay flyer out of the *Vancouver Province* newspaper. Grandfather resumes reading the *Northern Miner*, now sporting a burn hole through it. He rubs his fallen pipe ashes into the car-pet as I marvel at Milton Caniff's drawings of DC3s and P40s conducting the Burma campaign in the funny papers.

Part of Ontario was now showing through the cloud cover, and it looked quite innocent of the charges previously laid. Peering out through the arcing propeller, I noted that the blades were now catching the orange glint of a setting sun as I dialled up the Thunder

Bay ADIS. "Advise Thunder Bay tower, you have information Foxtrot," squawked the recorded message, and then it recycled, telling me the runway in use and the local weather. I quickly checked the approach plate information to visualize the look of the airport in order to find my way around, then spotted it ten miles dead ahead. Enright and his CBC were history, they had done their job. I switched them off and called Thunder Bay Radio with a position report. In a few minutes my wheels yelped on the runway of my grandfather's birthplace. He would be pleased but would still insist I head north, where Canada's future lies.

The morning dawned, and my hotel window looked like the TV set I left on all night—snow. Everybody was ticked off with me, sitting here in Thunder Bay, running up a hotel and restaurant bill that would choke a horse.

"Have you tried heading down the lake into the States?" asked the chief pilot, on the second day I was storm-bound. "Not a chance," I replied. "Nothing is moving out of here, not even IFR traffic. It's a blinding snow storm."

"Okay," said the voice over the phone, "but get out of there as soon as you can." I acknowledged and hung up. The food at the hotel was uninspiring, and I wanted to move as badly as my

employers wanted me to move, but the entire Lake Ontario area was blotto. Even the roads were closed from ice storms.

On the third day, it lifted. Sault Ste. Marie was reporting "severe clear," while the rest of the country was generally three thousand feet, with variable visibility due to local snow flurries. I was airborne in the early morning, tracking the lakeshore to White River, where I ran into a doozer of a local squall, bringing visibility down to zilch again. I checked with Sault Ste. Marie Radio and received confirmation that they were clear and visibility was unlimited.

The thought of returning to that hotel food, despite the sexy waitress, made me do something I'd never done before in my flying career: I punched it. "Punching it" is an expression to describe climbing through the overcast and into the blue (you hope). Never mind that it isn't legal; it isn't even sensible, but the pressure of all those company people waiting for their airplane and trying to get this idiot off their payroll drove me to it.

But what I thought would be a few thousand feet through the clag turned into 12,500 feet. I actually broke out at nine thousand and was faced with an inclined plane of cloud ahead of me. I climbed up the inclined plane and topped it at 12,500 feet, zinging along in this blue sky without a block air space clearance, as if I knew what I was doing. I kept swivelling my head around, checking every position on the clock to make sure I was alone. In twenty minutes I was over Montreal Island, in the clear, letting down for the Canadian Soo. The pucker factor was high, but for the rest of the trip into Brantford it was clear sailing.

When I rolled to a stop on the taxiway at Brantford's airport and shut down those reliable little engines, I sat for a few moments in the cockpit, listening to the sounds with which every pilot is familiar: the whine of the gyros spinning down and the "click" of cooling cylinders. I knew my commercial flying days were near their close, and I was savouring this moment as one of my most memorable experiences.

It had been an appropriate consummation of a forty-year love affair with airplanes, having flown across the country that my pioneer ancestors had helped to build, retracing their path from above and seeing the breadth of the land they had helped to shape. As I climbed out of this fine airplane, I was a different person from the man who had boarded it in Dawson City only a few flying hours earlier.

BC AIRLINES LTD

JUSTIN de GOUTIERE

PATHLESS WAY

DAVE HANNAY ·

· DAVE HILL ·

· TONEY WILSON ·

· BILL WADDINGTON ·

·EDMUNSON·

· DARRYL BROWN ·

· BLACK·   Y

· NED FRANCIS ·

· BILL GREEN ·